Redefining University Leadership for the 21st Century

Authored by:

Christina Chow
RMIT University, Melbourne, Australia

&

Clement Leung
Victoria University, Australia

Redefining University Leadership for the 21st Century

Authors: Christina Chow and Clement Leung

ISBN (Online): 978-1-68108-749-8

ISBN (Print): 978-1-68108-750-4

© 2018, Bentham eBooks imprint.

Published by Bentham Science Publishers – Sharjah, UAE. All Rights Reserved.

First published in 2018.

General:

1. Any dispute or claim arising out of or in connection with this License Agreement or the Work (including non-contractual disputes or claims) will be governed by and construed in accordance with the laws of the U.A.E. as applied in the Emirate of Dubai. Each party agrees that the courts of the Emirate of Dubai shall have exclusive jurisdiction to settle any dispute or claim arising out of or in connection with this License Agreement or the Work (including non-contractual disputes or claims).
2. Your rights under this License Agreement will automatically terminate without notice and without the need for a court order if at any point you breach any terms of this License Agreement. In no event will any delay or failure by Bentham Science Publishers in enforcing your compliance with this License Agreement constitute a waiver of any of its rights.
3. You acknowledge that you have read this License Agreement, and agree to be bound by its terms and conditions. To the extent that any other terms and conditions presented on any website of Bentham Science Publishers conflict with, or are inconsistent with, the terms and conditions set out in this License Agreement, you acknowledge that the terms and conditions set out in this License Agreement shall prevail.

Bentham Science Publishers Ltd.
Executive Suite Y - 2
PO Box 7917, Saif Zone
Sharjah, U.A.E.
Email: subscriptions@benthamscience.org

BENTHAM SCIENCE

CONTENTS

FOREWORD

This is the authors' second book on universities in the 21st century, and it couldn't come at a more relevant time, when public confidence in higher education is fading. With rising graduate unemployment, bloated administrative costs and student dissatisfaction, it's no surprise that people are questioning the value of a degree, not to mention the university's viability as an institution. If the essential work of teaching and research is to continue, the management model must change – and that begins with an honest examination of a university's function and purpose.

In this marvellously insightful book, the authors offer some valuable strategies to help university leaders and students succeed in this uncertain era, when technology and artificial intelligence make knowledge rapidly redundant. They show us how thinking and behaviour need to change, from the top down. This book gets to the heart of what makes a great university – and one that can survive.

Professor Alfredo Milani
University of Perugia
Italy

PREFACE

In our 2016 book, *Reshaping Universities for Survival in the 21st Century: New Opportunities and Paradigms*, we described the landscape of higher education and the challenges facing universities. We reflected on the unintended consequences of competition and marketization, such as ballooning student debt, graduate unemployment, and academic capitalism. In this follow-up book, we examine in greater detail the consequences of market failures caused by the marketization of higher education: an oversupply of graduates, the exploitation of PhD students for cheap labor, student dissatisfaction, the mismatch between qualifications and needed skills, student disillusionment, and the diminishing return on investments by students and their families. These failures have all contributed to society's loss of confidence in universities. The marketable "excellence" of universities is artificially based on ranking metrics which neglect the core academic mission of teaching. The volume of research produced has had poor outcomes and only served to enhance ranking metrics. Poor management and bloated administration are major causes of high fees and student unaffordability. While student demand declines in the West, China strives to be the world's new science superpower. Meanwhile, there is the omnipresent threat of disruption by new technologies.

In our narrative, our purpose has been to search for the quintessence of the idea of a university, the key principle which has enabled the institution to survive. We explain how universities can future-proof university graduates in this fast-changing world and contribute to the public good. We argue that the old managerial models are incompatible with the volatile, uncertain, complex and ambiguous world (VUCA) we now face. Finally, we offer strategies for university leaders to lead effectively in the VUCA era, illustrated by a case study.

Christina Chow
RMIT University
Melbourne
Australia

&

Clement Leung
United International College
China and Victoria University
Melbourne
Australia

ABOUT THE AUTHORS

Dr. Christina Chow *has an Honours degree in Microbiology and Immunology from Canada's McGill University, a Master of Management from the Norwegian School of Management, and a Doctor of Business Administration from the University of Newcastle, Australia. She is a Fellow of the Australian Institute of Company Directors, a Fellow of the Australian Institute of Management, and a member of Ausbiotech. She has teaching, research and management experience at institutions including McGill University, University of Hong Kong, University of Melbourne, Royal Children's Hospital and RMIT University. She also has extensive experience in corporate governance and financial, project and risk management in the tertiary education sector. At RMIT University in Australia, she has worked with the former Vice-Chancellor and Chancellor in establishing RMIT's Campus in Vietnam, the first foreign-owned campus in the country and Australia's largest offshore campus. She is currently the Principal Advisor in Global Business in the College of Science, Engineering & Health at RMIT University. Her previous publication includes "Mission Possible? An analysis of Australian universities' missions" and "Reshaping Universities for Survival in the 21st Century: New Opportunities and Paradigms".*

Professor Clement Leung's *academic experience spans four continents. Professor Leung obtained his BSc (Hons) in Mathematics from McGill University, Canada, an MSc in Mathematics from Oxford University, and a PhD in Computer Science from University College London. He has an outstanding record of research achievements and extensive experience in the building up of academic units and international engagement. He has held several academic appointments in Europe, including an Established Chair and Head of Department at the University of London. His Australasian academic appointments include the Foundation Chair in Computer Science at Australia's Victoria University, and full professorships at the National University of Singapore and Hong Kong Baptist University. He holds two US patents, and his publications include four books and well over one hundred research articles in top high-impact journals. His services to the academic community include serving as Program Chair, Program Co-Chair, Keynote Speaker, Panel Expert, and on the Program Committee and Steering Committee of major International Conferences. In addition to serving on the Editorial Board of ten international journals, he has served as Chairman of the International Association for Pattern Recognition Technical Committee on Multimedia and Visual Information Systems, as well as well as on the International Standards (ISO) MPEG-7 Committee responsible for generating standards for digital multimedia, where he played an active role in shaping the influential MPEG-7 International Standard. He is listed in Who's Who in Australia, Who's Who in the World, Great Minds of the 21st Century, Dictionary of International Biography, and Who's Who in Australasia & Pacific Nations. He is a Fellow of the British Computer Society, awarded a Chartered Fellow by the British Computer Society, and a Fellow of the Royal Society of Arts, Manufactures and Commerce.*

ACKNOWLEDGEMENTS

Any historical, critical and integrative research depends on the research, analyses and observations of previous scholars. We are greatly indebted to each and every source cited in this eBook and we hope that we have made every effort to cite them appropriately.

We are very grateful for the expert advice of the staff at Bentham science eBook Department, especially for the tireless support and guidance of Ms. Humaira Hashmi, Editorial Manager of Publications and Ms. Hira Aftab, Assistant Manager, eBooks Publications Department.

CONSENT FOR PUBLICATION

Not applicable.

CONFLICT OF INTEREST

The authors confirm that the authors have no conflict of interest to declare for this publication.

CHAPTER 1

A Sign of the Times

Abstract: This chapter looks at the negative headlines that currently dominate the public image of universities. In a climate of increasing graduate unemployment and underemployment and ever-increasing fees, the public is questioning the real value of a higher education. The crisis in college costs is eroding the democratic promise of higher education.

Keywords: College affordability and access, Graduate unemployment and underemployment, Howard Bowen's revenue theory of costs.

Today, the Western university model is under near-constant attack. Barely a week goes by without a broadsheet launching a scathing critique of Western university culture: the prevailing narrative is that this is a system in decay. Negative headlines dominate the public image of universities: "We've turned our unis into aimless, moneygrubbing exploiters of students" (Gittens 2017, The Sydney Morning Herald); "Are universities worth it?" (Aedy *et al.* 2017, Australian Broadcasting Corporation); "Degrees of failure: why it's time to reconsider how we run our universities" (Wolf 2017, Prospect Magazine UK); "Universities are broke. So let's cut the pointless admin and get back to teaching" (Spicer 2017, The Guardian UK); "University tuition fees are a pointless Ponzi scheme" (Swinford & Turner 2017, The Telegraph UK) "Is the Knowledge Factory broken?" (BBC The Inquiry 2017); "Is the public really losing faith in higher education?" (Lederman 2017, Inside Higher Education); "Moody's Downgrades Higher Ed's Outlook From 'Stable' to 'Negative'" (Harris 2017, The Chronicle of Higher Education); "The Case against Education: Why the Education System Is a Waste of Time and Money" (Caplan, 2018).

These headlines signal a worrying trend. It is hard to imagine that in our 21ˢᵗ century knowledge economy, the demand for higher education and lifelong learning could lead to anything but growth. With the support of advanced technologies, higher education has enormous potential for expansion, in terms of providing wider access, improved quality, and greater affordability. Instead, universities have morphed into businesses heavily focused on rankings and league tables, with ever-increasing fees becoming an issue for the majority of students. It is not surprising that, in this climate of increasing graduate unemployment and underemployment, the public is questioning the real value of a higher education.

Higher education is a critical factor for achieving social mobility in society. This is the basis of the American Dream: that one can realise one's potential through a good education and hard work. Unfortunately, access to higher education is now out of reach for low-income families. In fact, the Institute for Higher Education Policy report has found that 95% of US colleges are unaffordable for low-income students (Poutré, Rorison, & Voight 2017). Most Americans cannot keep up with the escalating costs of a university education.

Yet universities seem oblivious to the rising dissatisfaction in society. While many industries such as health, aviation and manufacturing have progressed to take advantage of new technologies and management methods to better service their customers, most universities have retreated back to their bureaucratic ivory towers. Few current leaders have the courage to break ranks and demystify the marketization of universities or discuss the real purpose of higher education. Many administrators name-check values which happen to be in vogue – student experience, student outcomes, student entrepreneurialism – without putting their resources towards providing the transformational experience that students need. Instead, they seem focused on short-term goals, such as increasing student enrolment numbers for the next semester.

In 2017, Dr. Michael Poliakoff, President of the American Council of Trustees and Alumni (ACTA) said that universities' ballooning administrative costs are a huge impediment to college affordability and access (American Council of Trustees and Alumni 2017). This is bad for morale. A recent report by the Institute for Higher Education Policy found that, even with the maximum level of federal financial aid, 70% of universities are unaffordable for the majority of students. The crisis in college costs is eroding the democratic promise of higher education.

The amount of funds spent on teaching *versus* administration reflects a university's priorities and its institutional efficiency. A 2010 study of higher education costs in the United States found that there was a 39% increase in teaching expenditure per student between 1993 and 2007, compared to a 61% increase in administrative spending per student. Again, a 2014 report found that the ratio of academics to administrators at public research universities in the US had declined from 3.5 in 1990 to 2.7 in 2000. By 2012, the ratio had dropped again, to 2.2 (Archibald & Feldman 2008). This explosion of university administrators, while cutting back on academic staff, does not make rational sense to observers.

Based on Howard Bowen's "revenue theory of costs" (Bowen 1980), the problem of cost escalation could be due to the rising revenue made available to universities, which tend to spend all the funds they can raise. According to this model, revenue becomes the driver of cost, rather than cost being a determinant of tuition. Furthermore, some universities set fees according to what they think students are willing to pay: a figure established by comparison with their ranked competitors and the public perception of excellence.

CHAPTER 2

Contrived Excellence

Abstract: This chapter looks at the manufactured excellence of universities which are based on league tables and ranking metrics. Success in these rankings lulls universities into a false sense of security and complacency. Societies are beginning to feel that universities which run as businesses and are obsessed with growing revenue cannot pursue real learning. There is declining confidence even within the higher education sector. Such negative sentiments have wider implications, as politicians can use them as an excuse in cutting government funding and attacking universities and experts.

Keywords: Academic Dishonesty, Cheating, Dropout Rates, Plagiarism, Student-Centric Learning, Testamur Forgeries.

Sir Keith Burnett, Vice-Chancellor of the University of Sheffield, has declared that "universities are becoming like mechanical nightingales". He likens the current predicament of universities to Hans Christian Andersen's story of the emperor who was captivated by an artificial mechanical nightingale instead of a real bird. Although the mechanical bird has some of the ideals of a perfect bird, it has a limited repertoire of songs and cannot fly. In the end, the emperor falls ill and is rescued by the real bird and its genuine singing abilities. Burnett's point is that universities have constructed an artificial model of excellence metrics which ignore the real purposes of education. Instead of serving the needs of society and the mission of scholarship, they are now focused primarily on achieving high ranks in league tables. Success in these rankings lulls them into a false sense of security and complacency (Burnett 2016).

Academic faculties experience the same kind of frustration as the students and the general public. Sadly, universities have been taken over by the worst elements of corporate culture and commercial agenda: exploiting staff, short-changing students, and dishonestly recruiting students into disciplines which have no job outcomes. However, many university heads would deny that such a crisis of confidence even exists; endless funding fights with governments are distracting them from the mission of education. Universities are accused of giving lavish executive salaries to a parade of senior university leaders, while crying poor in the face of funding cuts. The excessive remuneration given to university vice-chancellors has recently come under the spotlight in Australia and the UK, with education ministers calling for restraints. At the same time, universities are exploiting their sessional teachers and PhD students, who shoulder a large proportion of teaching responsibilities.

Although students now pay higher tuition fees, they appear to be putting less effort into their studies, leading to high dropout rates – for instance, Australian universities are experiencing their lowest completion rates since the time series began in 2005. In the 2010 cohort, only 66 percent of students had completed a course after six years. That rate is even worse for students studying for a degree in teaching, where the completion rate has dropped to 62% (Australian Government Department of Education 2017). Some Australian universities reported that dropout rates for first-year students were as high as 40%, with the average hovering around 21%. There are also concerns about the growing number of students who reported that they were not fully utilizing their skills and education three years after graduation (Australian Government Department of Education 2017). In the UK, the Higher Education Statistics Agency (HESA) reports that for first-degree students aged under 21 who enrolled in 2013-14, the dropout rate was 6% after one year of studies, with some universities' dropout rates reaching 20%. Similarly, in the US, the dropout rates of many four-year institutions are approaching 50%, with dropout at two-year colleges reaching as high as 80% (Craig 2017).

In the first two decades of the 21ˢᵗ century, universities in the West have enjoyed unprecedented growth in terms of numbers. International student enrolments have boomed. Cities have an explosion of new campus buildings. Almost every major university has an ambitious master plan to expand its footprint, sometimes creating campuses in cities which are depressed (Wolf 2017). Is this expansion frenzy sustainable? Are universities living on borrowed money? In a depressed employment environment, it is not realistic to expect that students can continue to shoulder the huge financial burdens. At the same time, the home countries of international students are rapidly building better universities. In the past decade, many universities have adopted expansion as a key part of their innovation agenda. However, it is time we examined the unrestrained expansion of universities.

As institutions of higher learning, have universities forgotten that one of their primary missions is to help students learn, to have life-changing experiences, and to continue on a journey of lifelong learning? With all the zest for industry engagement, innovation and commercialisation, students seem to have been omitted from a university's success formula (Featherstone 2016). Regrettably, universities are preoccupied with increasing student revenue and recruiting high profile researchers in order to boost their global university rankings. Students and teaching-dedicated academics are not a priority, except when student survey results are released. Institutions may pay lip service to student-centric learning, but they rarely investigate how to actually improve the experience of genuine learning. There is a great deal that universities can do to help the new generation of students accommodate learning into their lifestyles, such as the use of virtual reality and artificial intelligence.

Societies are beginning to feel that universities which run as businesses and are obsessed with growing revenue cannot pursue real learning (Gillings & Williamson 2015). There are widespread cases of cheating, plagiarism, academic dishonesty, testamur forgeries and a general decline in academic standards reported in Australian universities – even the most elite institutions are not immune to this phenomenon. An open market exists for selling assignments and essay-writing services. Alarmingly, some final-year medical students were found to have falsified records of interviews with patients who had died, in order to pass their assignments (Gillings & Williamson 2015). The intention of the exercise was to help students better understand the plight of patients with chronic medical conditions; however, these students were not interested to learn and had no respect for the integrity of the profession.

In this climate, one cannot be sure of the quality of graduates produced by the system. There is little wonder that employers complain about the lack of appropriate skills in graduates. In their appetite for ever-increasing student revenue, some universities are admitting students who are unsuited to higher learning, and merely require a diploma for career purposes. For these students, a degree is little more than an accessory; they do not care about professional integrity or doing justice to their fellow graduates. Lamentably, universities fail to instil in their students a desire for learning: the primary responsibility of higher education.

The truth is that corporatized and partially-privatised universities in Australia have become addicted to fee-paying students, especially those from overseas who pay higher fees to secure their places. While the excuse is that they need to compensate for the lack of adequate government funding, there is no real justification for the insatiable appetite for revenue. Universities often accept borderline overseas students in order to achieve their revenue targets. This unbridled growth, sanctioned by the Government, creates a race to the bottom, putting the integrity of all universities at risk. If universities were to be put under stress-tests (like those applied in the banking sector where a simulation is used to see if an institution can remain solvent under difficult financial situations), they would be in great financial stress given any significant drop in international student enrolments.

There is declining confidence even within the higher education sector. In a report released by the Chronicle of Higher Education, the percentage of academic leaders in the US who regard American universities as the best or among the best in the world has fallen dramatically, from 87% to 67% from 2014 to 2017. The percentage of academic leaders who believe that the US will remain a leading force in higher education has also dropped, from 78% in 2014 to 60% in 2017.

A 2017 survey of US College Chief Business Officers by Inside Higher Ed (Lederman & Seltzer 2017) reveals that 71% of the respondents are increasingly concerned about the financial stability of US colleges. That figure is up from 63% in 2016 and 56% in 2015. These business officers said that universities would most likely respond by boosting student enrolments. There was also conjecture that institutions might merge, consolidate or use shared services. Given the declining number of potential domestic students in the US, some business officers voiced concerns that the large number of colleges and universities in the country is unsustainable.

Some universities are aggressively looking for international students to fill the revenue gaps. The financial stress of US public and private four-year institutions is confirmed by the latest credit rating released by Moody, which changed its outlook for the sector from "stable" to "negative." (Harris 2017). Moody cited muted growth in tuition revenue and uncertainty surrounding the federal government policy changes as grounds for its downgrade. In January 2018, the ratings agency Standard and Poor's gave a bleak outlook for the US higher education sector. The agency listed the recently passed tax reform and its uncertain impact on the endowment of institutions as one of the reasons for its negative rating. The agency believes that many institutions have limited flexibility and resources to draw on in the face of further credit pressure. The agency also cited the growing disconnect between students' expectations of better employment outcomes and their willingness to pay would put greater strain on mid-level institutions (Harris 2018).

The distrust of so-called expertise is another symptom of the declining confidence in universities. Experts claim that their expertise based on training and years of research, usually conducted at universities and through teaching and consultancy experience. Yet many politicians have publicly disdained such authority. Michael Gove, the former British Secretary of State for Justice, famously stated during a debate on Brexit that "people in this country have had enough of experts" (Mance 2016). It appears that the public is still harboring a grievance towards experts for not being able to predict the Global Financial Crisis of 2007 (Clark 2017). The erosion of public confidence in universities is affecting philanthropic donations to these once-revered institutions.

Recently, a Pew Research Center study (2017) found that while 55% of the US public continued to regard universities as having a positive effect on the country, Republican voters had increasingly negative views on the national institutions. In 2017, 58% of Republicans and Republican-leaning independents said that colleges and universities have a negative effect on the country. This sentiment might have contributed to the delay in the re-authorisation of the Higher Education Act by the US Congress. The declining perception of universities could be due to problems of affordability and ballooning student debts, as well as the debate over freedom of expression. There has been growing dissatisfaction over universities' handling of student protests, with the feeling that university presidents should uphold absolute freedom of expression at all costs (Arnett 2017). Controversies over disinviting and removing speakers, and the creation of safe spaces, has probably damaged the conservative perception of universities.

In fact, a 2016 Pew Research Center found that over 70% of Americans believed in protecting the views of those with unpopular opinions and the right to nonviolent protest, which they regard as crucial to democracy. Further surveys conducted in the late 2017 by the Wall Street Journal, NBC News, Civis Analytics and Echelon Insights found similar public sentiments towards higher education. It appears that Americans are losing faith in the value of a college degree. The research shows society's increasing doubt of the value of higher education, based on the fear of a huge debt burden and the slim chance of finding a well-paid job. Some respondents felt that universities were more concerned in pushing their own agenda and a particular political viewpoint, rather than focusing on useful subject matter and real-world skills (Lederman 2017). These negative sentiments have wider implications, as politicians can use them as an excuse in cutting government funding and attacking universities and experts.

One of the more damning reports on the current state of higher education comes from the United Kingdom. In December 2017, the UK National Audit Office released a report (Morse 2017) highly critical of its Higher Education market. It was prepared by Sir Amyas Morse KCB, Comptroller and Auditor General for the House of Commons. The report found that over the past few decades, the UK Government has increasingly relied on market mechanisms for the delivery of its national higher education. The intention was supposedly to give students more choices and create greater competition among providers in order to improve quality, deliver better value for money and reduce social inequity. Regrettably, the audit found that the marketization of higher education in UK had failed to deliver the intended outcomes.

The report found that the UK Government has made huge investments in its higher education system. The UK Department of Education increased the upfront funding for higher education from £6 billion in 2007/08 to over £9 billion a year in 2016, with funding per undergraduate increasing from £5,381 to £7,903 at 2016 prices. UK students pay for their higher education through income-contingent repayment loans, with a legal obligation to make repayments based on earnings after completing their studies. Any unpaid student loan balance is written off after 30 years and the Department estimates that around 40–45% of the student loans will never be repaid. Despite these massive investments, the outcomes have been very disappointing. Among the key findings, the report found that:

"Only 32% of students from England consider their course offers value for money, down from 50% in 2012. This figure is the lowest in the UK. Furthermore, 37% of students from England consider their course poor value" (Key Finding 15).

The audit also found that:

"Higher education has a more limited level of consumer protection than other complex products such as financial services ………. Prospective students have very little access to independent advice" (Key Finding 11).

The report went on to explain:

"Prospective students are in a potentially vulnerable position when deciding whether to enter higher education and take on a student loan. Higher education involves a potentially significant financial commitment, unlike other options such as apprenticeships. The average student debt, for a three-year course, on graduation is £50,000. This represents a legal financial liability, and is one of the largest financial commitments most students will make in their lives. It is likely to be second in scale only to mortgages which average £139,000 in the UK. Research in 2016 found that 58% of 15- to 18-year-olds, the typical age at which decisions on higher education are made, had not received any form of financial education that would improve their financial capability and numeracy to help protect them from making poor choices. The Financial Conduct Authority, which regulates financial service firms, identifies financial capability as one of the key drivers of vulnerability" (Key Finding 10).

Furthermore, the audit found that there is no meaningful price competition in the sector to drive down prices for the benefit of the student and taxpayer (Key Finding 16), and that *"market incentives for higher education providers to compete for students on course quality are weak"* (Key Finding 17). Moreover, *"students can do little to influence quality once on a course, despite improvements in complaints handling"* (Key Finding 18), and *"there is not yet evidence that more providers entering and exiting the market will improve quality in the sector, and protections for students are untested*" (Key Finding 19). In conclusion, universities would be accused of "mis-selling" if they were in the financial sector, and there is definitely a market failure in higher education in the UK. In response to the audit report, Meg Hillier, the Member of Parliament who chairs the Public Accounts Committee, said that "the Government had created a generation of students hit by massive debts, many of whom doubt their degree is worth the money paid for it" (Richardson BBC 2017).

CHAPTER 3

Managerial Malaise

Abstract: Ballooning administrative costs in universities are a huge impediment to college affordability and access. Not only is over-bloated administration bad for institutional morale, it is sapping the energy and vitality of universities. Excessive administration poses the greatest threat to the existence of universities.

Keywords: Administrative Blight, Conflict of Interest, Social Contract.

It is widely recognised that ballooning administrative costs in universities are a huge impediment to college affordability and access. Not only is over-bloated administration bad for institutional morale, it is sapping the energy and vitality of universities. While managers and administrators are pre-occupied with endless meetings, workshops, and planning retreats, purporting to manage the operational business of the university, they are distracting from and interfering with real academic work. By using management buzz words such as bench marking, best practice, and Key Performance Indicators, they ceaselessly demand progress reports from the faculty. As many of these professional administrators have no academic experience, they see managing as an end in itself. Yet, many administrators do not even carry out these management tasks, instead they outsource them to external consultants who engage in real problem-solving for universities. Hence, we see that much of the higher education research is actually performed by consultancy companies.

While the main purposes of a university are teaching and research, many professional managers have little understanding of these academic missions. They have no stake in catering to the needs of students or in pursuing the university's academic aspirations. They may come up with ostentatious ideas to distract the university from its missions to secure their own positions. Protecting the university's resources and reputation is not necessarily a priority. They command outrageously high executive salary packages and make luxurious overseas trips, supposedly to promote internationalization. They enjoy the perks of corporate executives but without the corresponding responsibilities. Professor Ginsberg from Johns Hopkins University has called this phenomenon the *administrative blight* (Ginsberg 2011). In his book, *The Fall of the Faculty: The Rise of the All-Administrative University and Why It Matters*, he cites numerous examples of university managers squandering millions in acquiring the wrong IT systems, investing in failed projects, or worse still, lavishing money on themselves. Professor Ginsberg describes numerous cases of university managers who have taken advantage of their power and access: stealing, colluding, taking bribes and kickbacks, or even falsifying credentials in order to secure senior positions.

Ginsberg likens the growth of the university administration to a cancerous tumor – and he is not confident that a single form of treatment will cure the condition. However, a use of combined approaches could at least lengthen the life of the patient – in this case, the university. He proposes to use college affordability and productivity data to appeal to university governing boards. He suggests at least a 10% cut across the board on university administration, beginning with senior administrators. University governing boards are advised to benchmark their own universities with the national average. Boards must have tough rules against conflict-of-interest, as well as rigorous monitoring systems in place. They must resist submitting to management fads, which may be disguised grabs for power by the administrators. Professor Ginsberg believes that excessive administration poses the greatest threat to the existence of universities.

It is interesting to note that most elite Ivy League universities do not have a high ratio of administrators to academics. It may be that lower-ranked universities expend a great deal on administration in their attempt to emulate the top universities. In July 2017, the American Council of Trustees and Alumni and the Institute for Effective Governance released a guide for higher education trustees, titled *How Much is Too Much? Controlling Administrative Costs through Effective Oversight.* It recommends that governing boards take a more active role in monitoring and controlling ballooning administrative costs in universities. As excessive administrative costs are a huge barrier to college affordability, every university has an obligation to deliver the best possible education at the lowest possible cost. At some colleges, administrative costs have far exceeded those of the faculty, with administrators earning three to five times as much as professors. Not only is this bad for "optics" – it is also very bad for academic morale.

Recruitment search firms are a considerable part of the problem, since they encourage bidding wars for administrative professionals. Governing boards should compel their administrators to shift spending priorities away from management towards the core business of the universities: teaching and research. Professor Ginsberg says that a 10% cut in management ranks may not be sufficient to improve university operations; however, he believes that a 20% cut in management would produce significant and observable benefits. Furthermore, universities should be judicious in expending donations and gifts. It would be useful if donations were earmarked for academic pursuits, rather than being put into general purpose funds which could be raided by administrators.

In July 2017, the Higher Education Funding Council, the lead regulator for England's university sector, received a complaint alleging poor governance process with regard to the excessive remuneration of senior leaders at the University of Bath. After due investigation, the Council issued a report, which was highly critical of University of Bath's governance process and the management of issues relating to conflict of interest. In November 2017, the vice-chancellor of the University of Bath, was forced to step down amid student protests and a furore over accusations of excessive pay. However, compared with the salaries given to vice-chancellors at Australian universities, the vice-chancellor of the University of Bath's salary is at the low end! (Coughlan 2017; The Guardian 2018).

Undoubtedly, there is a crisis of confidence here, with the public questioning the role of universities in society. Are universities fulfilling their social contract? National governments are ignoring universities' calls for ever-more funding, pointing out that universities are continually increasing tuition fees while failing to cut down on bloated administration and executive payments. Governments want more transparent accountability, but this idea is abhorrent to most universities, who adhere to a notion of institutional autonomy and object to any semblance of political interference. In their struggle to gain financial independence, universities in the UK, Australia and USA are leading the charge towards greater privatization and marketization. But is this unbridled marketization sustainable? There will be dire consequences when the bubble finally bursts. Professor Clayton Christensen of Harvard Business School predicts that by 2028, half of US universities will be heading for bankruptcy. He is not alone. "Thirty years from now, the big university campuses will be relics. Universities won't survive," wrote Peter Drucker, one of the founders of modern management, in 1997 (Kenzner & Johnson 1997). Forbes Magazine flags "Disruption: Coming Soon to a University Near You" (Fischer 2012). In Pearson's publication "An avalanche is coming: Higher education and the revolution ahead", writers conclude that "the 20th century models of universities are broken. Unless universities are transformed, an avalanche will sweep the system away" (Barber *et al.* 2013). The *Economist* has repeatedly warned that "a cost crisis, changing labour markets and new technology will turn an old institution on its head" and that "the staid higher-education business is about to experience a welcome earthquake" (Economist 2014).

CHAPTER 4

Is the Knowledge Factory Broken?

Abstract: Universities value research above teaching due to its influence on ranking tables. Many universities tend to offer high-margin programs in order to channel teaching surpluses towards funding research. Mediocre researchers are valued over inspiring teachers, who are often passed over for promotion. The existence of a research-teaching nexus is questionable when most researchers hardly teach. Despite the proliferation of research publications, groundbreaking research has actually decreased in the last few decades. There are claims that most published research is false, and that there is a crisis of credibility due to the inability to replicate many experiments.

Keywords: Australian Productivity Commission, Incentive System, *P-hacking*, Research-Teaching Nexus.

Many universities value research above teaching due to its influence on ranking tables. According to the 2017 Australian Productivity Commission report *Shifting the Dial*, many universities tend to offer high-margin programs in order to channel teaching surpluses towards funding research. Mediocre researchers are valued over inspiring teachers, who are often passed over for promotion. The existence of a research-teaching nexus is questionable when most researchers hardly teach. While billions and billions of dollars have been spent on research, there is not much to show for these huge investments. In short, the preoccupation with research has yielded few results. Despite the proliferation of research publications, groundbreaking research has actually decreased in the last few decades. Even the peer-review process of prestige journals has come into question. While national governments spend millions in administering research ranking exercises, some researchers try to game the system by citing the same publications multiple times, using different first authors or titles. Some have even admitted to exaggerating and overrating the possible impact of their work. On the other hand, good researchers are forced to spend more time applying for grants than doing actual research.

The fundamental problem is a perverse incentive system which rewards quantity rather than quality of publications. In some areas of research, the majority of the work does not even meet reasonable standards of statistical rigor, since it will only be read by the editors and the investigators.

In a recent episode of BBC's *The Inquiry* ("Is the Knowledge Factory broken?", 2017), the production of academic research was put under the microscope. The current controversies surrounding research findings revolve around the claims that most published research is false, and that there is a crisis of credibility due to the inability to replicate many experiments. Academic research – which is the heart of the university mission – is accused of producing useless and dubious data. In *The Inquiry*, some critics say that 40% of medical procedures based on research findings are either useless or have the potential to cause harm. Many research projects are accused of lacking real-world relevance and being downright frivolous, serving only to game the research-ranking system. There are even claims by academics that almost 90% of research published in top journals is not reproducible, with some famous scientists unable to reproduce their own published work. However, according to *The Inquiry*, these revelations have been hushed up. This is concerning, since huge efforts and funds have been poured into university research.

However, Fanelli (2018) asserted that the problem of the reproducibility crisis in science is exaggerated and not empirically supported, and does not accurately represent the general population of practicing scientists. While surveys have found some significant incidences of selective reporting, scientific misconduct and questionable research practices often influenced by the pressure to publish, such generalizations are unjustified, based on evidence from further meta-research studies. The author argued that the occurrence of questionable results may not be due to outright scientific misconduct but probably due to *P-hacking*, in which researchers select data or statistical analyses to make non-significant results become significant (Wicherts *et al.* 2016) While *P-hacking* is widespread, the phenomenon is not believed to have radically altered scientific consensus based on meta-analyses (Head *et al.* 2015, Fanelli 2018).

On the other hand, good research has not been put to efficient use for the public good. One explanation why society did not make better use of the vast amount of research generated was a lack of coherence. Some critics describe this as a "Tower of Babel" effect, where specialists from different disciplines are locked into their own hyper-specific languages and unable to communicate with one other. There is less interest in knowledge dissemination and collaboration for the public good than in demonstrating superiority in the speciality concerned.

There is a bias towards high-profile research that attracts positive attention and good publicity for universities. Instead of protecting academic freedom, many leaders today are concerned with their university's brand and image, to the extent that they determine and control the kind of research their academics conduct. In their haste to communicate showy research findings and generate positive publicity, they do not allow adequate time for rigorous peer review and self-correction. Research that seems "exciting" – that is, likely to attract good publicity and funding – is favoured, while research that has the potential to generate controversy is avoided. The desire to protect a university's brand inhibits the freedom to research, which is diametrically opposite to the concept of academic freedom.

In a climate that rewards superficiality over substance and rigor, there is little wonder that the amount of unreliable research continues to grow. This reflects poorly on general scientific practice and undermines public confidence in research as a whole – including the actual ground-breaking research which is taking place. Through training and mentorship, universities should be instrumental in fostering the highest standards of research practice to ensure the integrity and reliability of research activities and outputs. They should encourage openness and tolerance for honest errors, rather than pursuing quick wins and premature findings.

CHAPTER 5

The PhD – Glut or Ponzi Pyramid Scheme?

Abstract: The marketization of knowledge has led to an oversupply of PhD graduates, as it does not follow the economics of supply and demand. While industries continue to complain that PhD graduates lack appropriate knowledge and skills, universities exploit their PhD students as cheap labor for teaching and research activities. PhD students have become part of the flexible workforce to meet the universities' temporary workforce needs on a part-time and casual basis. As a result, universities tend to take on an excessive number of PhD students.

Keywords: Flexible Workforce, PhD Factory, Scientific Century, Transferrable Skills.

In today's post-industrial economy, the foundation for a nation's wealth creation are knowledge, research, creativity and innovation. Modern economies need high-level research scientists to create new knowledge, products, and technologies. In theory, a nation's PhD output is an indication of its research manpower resources. However, the trend towards marketizing knowledge has led to an oversupply of PhD graduates, which does not follow the economics of supply and demand from universities and industries. Industries continue to complain that PhD graduates lack appropriate knowledge and skills.

The title of the degree Doctor of Philosophy has its roots in the Middle Ages, but the current concept of the PhD dates back to the model of the Humboldtian university in the German tradition. However, the name of the degree is a little misleading. In medieval times, the degree was awarded for advanced scholarship rather than research, and was used in many disciplines and fields of study besides philosophy and theology (Noble 1994). It was the highest degree a scholar could attain in a chosen discipline. The word *philosophy* implied that the holders of the degree possessed advanced disciplinary knowledge, deep learning and understanding, wisdom and philosophical aspects of the discipline (Bourner, Bowden & Laing 2001). However, modern PhD training has little to do with the broader aspects of a discipline *per se*. In general, PhD training now tends towards narrow specialization. Newman cautioned that narrow minds would be the result of this narrow specialization (Ker 2008, Deboick 2010).

In 2012, the OECD called for more training in transferable skills for PhD candidates, who should be equipped with skills beyond their specific discipline for application in a broad variety of work situations. It recommends an industrial PhD, incorporating collaborative research with industries. In general, PhD training is beneficial to society and the production and dissemination of knowledge, and it is important to encourage talented students with the intellectual capacity and aptitude to pursue the degree. However, universities have quickly discovered that PhD students can carry out more research and deliver more teaching at a much lower cost than tenured staff. PhD students have become part of the "flexible workforce" – that is, they can meet the universities' temporary workforce needs on a part-time and casual basis. As a result, universities tend to take on an excessive number of PhD students, to the point where there is now an oversupply of PhD graduates. In other words, talented and hard-working PhD candidates have become a source of cheap labour for universities. Unconscionably, these talented students are exploited with the false promise of a bright career path.

Concern about the exploitation of PhD students is so widespread that the economist Professor Paula Stephan, of Georgia State University and a research associate at the National Bureau of Economic Research, likens the system to a Ponzi pyramid scheme (Stephan 2013). Many talented students find themselves faced with zero future academic prospects. With domestic PhD student numbers dwindling, many Western universities are taking on more overseas students, who are willing to carry out research and deliver teaching under lower payrates and less favourable conditions. Although PhD training can be an entry to a scientific career, most of PhD graduates end up in careers outside scientific research. A report by the UK's Royal Society, "The Scientific Century", found that only 3.5% of PhD graduates ended up with university research careers, and only 0.45 % reached the rank of full professor. In the long term, most graduates (80%) pursued a career outside scientific circles. The journal *Nature* has also raised the question of a PhD glut in the article "Education: The PhD factory. The world is producing more PhDs than ever before. Is it time to stop?" (Cyranoski *et al.* 2010).

The *Paris Innovation Review* (2014) has found that the number of PhD graduates increased dramatically, by nearly 40%, between 1998 and 2008 in OECD countries. The growth shows no sign of slowing. But the sad truth is that many of these PhD graduates may never get a chance to take full advantage of their training and qualifications. They are faced with declining prospects of tenured academic jobs, and an industrial sector that finds their skills irrelevant. Supply has finally outstripped demand. The problem is worst in Japan, since the country faces a low birth rate and an acute oversupply of PhD graduates. Japanese industries tend to prefer fresh young graduates who can be trained on the job. In 2009, the

Japanese government began offering companies around ¥4 million (US$47,000) to take on one of the country's 18,000 unemployed postdoctoral students.

China's PhD graduate numbers have also accelerated by more than 40% over a decade, to the point where it has overtaken the US to become the world's biggest producer of PhDs. The number of PhD holders in China is absurdly high, with some 146,941people graduating with doctorates across all disciplines in 2013. However, employment prospects for these domestic PhDs are declining, since universities and research institutes prefer to recruit those with foreign PhDs, while industries prefer to employ graduates with only a Master's degree at a lower cost. In Australia, the 2015 Postgraduate Destination report showed that PhD graduates had a much lower employment rate (72.7%) than those holding a Postgraduate Diploma (78.1%), Graduate Certificate (90.5 %), Coursework Masters (81.6 %), or Research Masters (79.6%). Some universities now offer supplementary entrepreneurship and management programs for their PhD graduates.

A 2010 *Economist* article, "Doctoral degrees: The disposable academic. Why doing a PhD is often a waste of time", reported serious exploitation problems in universities' research doctorates, in contrast to the practical "professional doctorates" in fields such as medicine, law, and business which have a more tangible value. In fact, a research PhD may even reduce one's earnings potential, offers no financial advantage or wage premium over a Master's degree. However, since most PhD programs are subsidised by national governments and students do not have to pay for PhD training, there is no price signal on the cost and benefits of the program. In addition, the dropout rate for PhD students can be as high as 50%. While the average time taken to complete a PhD is around four to five years, half of PhD candidates take ten years or more to complete their degrees.

Universities know full well that their PhD programs are overrated, but they continue to expanding these programs so that they can exploit talented students for cheap labour in research and teaching. Universities also get government funding from enrolling and completing PhD students. This is an enormous waste of talent and resources, not to mention the frustration, despair and sense of failure experienced by the students. The fiasco of the PhD program represents a failure in duty of care on the part of universities. They are culpable in deceptive conduct in promoting PhD programs but not taking their obligation to students seriously. Dialogue between governments, universities and industry is urgently needed to modify the training available in PhD programs. An industrial PhD, incorporating the skills needed by industry, offers an alternative to formal training programs at universities.

Fortunately, the PhD unemployment rate appears to have come down slightly since 2014 based on US Bureau of Labor Statistics. However, many of these PhD graduates still do not end up in an academic or research career. There are calls for transparency for PhD career outcomes (Benderly 2018 and Blank *et al.* 2017). Citing the case of biomedical PhDs, the authors warned that with the decline of US federal research funding by almost 20% from 2003 to 2016, and hyper-competition for academic positions, this means that only about 10% of biomedical trainees in the United States will find tenure-track positions at US institutions five years after completing a PhD. Similar concerns are growing around the world. For example, in the UK, only 3.5% of science PhDs will obtain an ongoing scientific research position in a university. In the US, the mismatch between the supply of biomedical doctoral students seeking academic appointments and available tenure-track positions is largely due to the lack of comprehensive data collected and disseminated to prospective PhD candidates. That mismatch in turn has contributed to a marked increase in the number of trainees spending years in postdoctoral fellowships, with few opportunities for advancement into academic and research positions.

CHAPTER 6

The Value of a University Education

Abstract: Human capital is a crucial element for industrialization. The post-industrial world relies heavily on knowledge as a vital part of economic growth. The supply of highly skilled workers trained through higher education is of increasing importance to the development of a nation's economy. A university education not only provides significant economic and non-monetary private benefits to students, it contributes substantial social and public benefits to society and future generations. However, critics argue that as decades of increasing access to higher education have not resulted in higher economic gains, the benefit of higher education could be in "signalling". Therefore, the critical question is whether the increasing social costs of higher education have produced a corresponding increase in social benefits. There is an ongoing debate among educational economists between the "signalling" effects *versus* the "developmental" effects of university education.

Keywords: Cultural Competence, International Diversity, Unified Growth Theories, Wage Premium.

Madsen & Murtin (2017) have demonstrated that education has been the most important driver of income growth in Britain from 1270 to 2010: that is, both before and after the first Industrial Revolution. Their findings give credence to the Unified Growth Theories, which state that human capital is a crucial element for industrialization.

In the current knowledge economy, the employability of individuals depends on their transportable knowledge and skills gained through a high level of education. Education improves economic productivity, standards and quality of life; it can enhance social mobility and equality, enriching the life of communities. The post-industrial world relies heavily on knowledge as a vital part of economic growth and development. As such, the supply of highly skilled workers who can create, disseminate and use knowledge acquired through higher education is of increasing importance to the development of a nation's economy (Edwards 2010).

A university education not only provides significant economic and non-monetary private benefits to students, it contributes substantial social and public benefits to society and future generations. Better-educated citizens are associated with a nation's higher productivity and economic growth, in addition to innovation and research outputs. It has been shown that there is a positive relationship between GDP per capita and education. This is why national governments feel the need to raise the education level of their citizens. In 2002, it was found that in the UK, a 1% increase in workers with higher education qualifications led to a 0.5% increase in GDP. Accordingly, it was projected that in 2016, the doubling of universities per capita should create a corresponding increase in GDP of 4%. However, in the last few years, we see a decline of productivity and a fall in GDP in developed countries. In the UK, US and Australia, where graduate numbers are rising, there is no evidence of any improvement in productivity. In fact, growth and productivity have been falling all over the world (Wolf, Sellen & Dominguez-Reig 2016). Higher education can no longer be a silver bullet to fix the world's economic woes.

Critics (Caplan 2018) show that decades of increasing access to higher education have not resulted in higher economic gains in the US. Caplan argues that a significant portion of the benefit of higher education is in "signalling". This means that employers use university education as a screening to identify prospective employees who have the ability and determination to complete a degree, even though the skills they acquired at university are not relevant to the work. Therefore, the critical question is whether the increasing social costs of higher education have produced a corresponding increase in social benefits. There is an ongoing debate among educational economists between the "signalling" effects *versus* the "developmental" effects of university education. Do degrees simply act as a filter for employers to easily identify brighter candidates, rather than those who actually benefited from the university experience?

There is mounting evidence of the un- and under-employment of graduates, accompanied by a falling graduate "wage premium". While there is an oversupply of graduates, employers are complaining of a widespread mismatch between skill shortages and the actual skills of job-seeking graduates. With the abundance of supply, some employers are driving credential inflation by demanding Bachelor's and Master's degrees as requirements for positions that do not need them. At the same time, other companies such as Ernst & Young, Penguin Random House, PriceWaterhouseCoopers, Ogilvy Group, Deloitte, Apple and Google have already relaxed their credential requirement, focusing on merit and abilities rather than relying on credentials from prestigious universities.

The 2017 UK Student Academic Experience Survey (Neves & Hillman 2017) found that university students have declining perceptions of value for money and report relatively low wellbeing compared to the rest of the population. Fees continue to be a pressing concern, and students are in favour of government contributing to the bulk of the cost. The proportion of students who feel they received good value from university education dropped from 37% to 35% over the previous year, while the proportion of those who feel they received poor value increased from 32% to 34%.

Global cultural competence and international diversity are two factors which are greatly valued by industry. However, most students do not perceive benefits in the internationalization of universities. Only 36% of students see clear advantages in interacting with international students, while a third are neutral, and the rest do not see any benefits.

The burning question for universities is whether we are teaching students enduring, employable skills. Are we preparing them for jobs which will be made rapidly obsolete by intelligent machines? How can universities help society address the industry disruptions which are reshaping our economy?

CHAPTER 7

A Diminishing Return on Investment

Abstract: In their zest for marketing, universities tend to over-promise and under-deliver. They are now being accused of short-changing their students. Studies have shown the falling value of a university degree. It has found a disconnect between employers' and recent graduates' perceptions of workforce preparedness.

Keywords: Anti-Science, Anti-Vaccination, Climate Sceptics, College Learning Assessment Plus (CLA+), Fake News, Participation Rate, "Post-Truth" Society, Smarts.

When making a substantial investment, one normally looks to measure the rate of return on money invested over a certain period. This measure allows investors to decide whether to undertake the investment and to compare the performance of different investments. When examining the performance of investing in a university program, some university degrees offer almost no return on investment while creating heavy student debt (Timothy 2017). The growth in graduate jobs has not kept up with the growth in the number of graduates. But this fact is not reflected in university marketing, which continues to sell a dream to prospective students. Michael Gove, former UK Secretary of State for Education and Secretary of State for Justice, describes university education as the ultimate "Ponzi scheme" and students are waking up to it (Timothy 2017).

In their zest for marketing, universities tend to over-promise and under-deliver. They are now being accused of short-changing their students, reducing face-to-face teaching to the minimum and discouraging students from attending classes on campus. Universities want to maximise their profit margin in teaching – partly to cross-subsidise research and partly to generate more discretionary funds. Admissions standards are lowered in order to ensure an increasing flow of international students, who may lack the communication skills to engage effectively in classes. The falling value of a university degree is shown in the latest Australian HILDA report (Wilkens 2017), which shows the deteriorating employment outcomes of university graduates. The Household, Income and Labour Dynamics in Australia (HILDA) Survey is funded by the Australian

Government Department of Social Services and is a nationally representative longitudinal study of Australian households. The declining employment outcomes of university graduates have prompted the question of whether graduates' skills are matching the employers' needs, or whether there are in fact too many graduates flooding the market. It is worth noting that since the lifting of the limit on enrolment numbers in 2008, domestic undergraduate student numbers in Australia have grown by a third (compared to a growth of 5% between 2001 and 2008). The HILDA Survey also found that there has been an increase in graduates pursuing further studies, as well as an increase in part-time employment (not combined with full-time study) amongst recent graduates. Consistent with the rise in part-time employment and decline in full-time employment, the average weekly earnings of new graduates have declined. However, it should be noted that the labour market outcomes for those without university education are significantly worse than those experienced by university graduates. The Australian Government has now suspended demand-driven funding from January 2018, and public funding for each Australian university will be frozen at the 2017 level for two years. A performance-based funding mechanism will also be introduced, in an attempt to address attrition rates and improve graduate outcomes.

A 2017 Wall Street Journal survey report found that in more than half of US colleges, a substantial number of final year university students scored below the basic level of critical thinking (Belkin 2017). The report was based on an analysis of results from the US College Learning Assessment Plus (CLA+), which is a critical-thinking test given annually to freshmen and seniors from around 200 US colleges. What this means is that while the students could generally read the test documents, they were unable to interpret the evidence presented and make a cohesive argument. This finding echoes earlier work by Richard Arum and Josipa Roska in their 2011 book *Academically Adrift: Limited Learning on College Campuses*. Arum and Roska (2011) showed that almost half of college students did not improve on important skills that they should have gained in their academic years in college. The authors convincingly argued that this problem was due to the lack of academic rigor at many universities. Students seemed to be drifting through college without a clear sense of purpose. Universities have oversold to students the notion of a higher education as a panacea and a guarantor of future success. Nevertheless, the higher education participation rate of most countries continues to rise, with the US reaching 34%, the UK 40%, Australia 37%, and Canada 32% (OECD 2015).

In the US, the 2016 PayScale and Future Workplace Report on Workforce-Skills Preparedness, "Leveling Up: How to Win In the Skills Economy", found a disconnect between employers' and recent graduates' perceptions of workforce preparedness. While the majority of graduate workers (87 percent) believed that they were well-prepared for their job upon graduation, 60 percent of managers felt they lacked critical thinking and problem-solving skills. In the same study, 44 percent of hiring managers felt that the graduates lacked writing proficiency, while 39 percent said that the graduates lacked public speaking skills.

Is critical thinking sufficient to enable graduates to do what their employers want? In fact, what employers value above all is the employee's ability to come up with new ideas and concepts, and to create innovative solutions to problems in order to beat the competition. They need what is popularly known as "smarts" (Leonard & Swap 2004). This means that they need more than reasoning and argumentation: they need to be able to use their intelligence to analyze and synthesize concepts. They need good judgement, strategic thinking, intuition, acumen, pattern recognition, design thinking, decision-making and fast problem-solving skills, all of which are needed to handle busy, complex work environments in real time.

While most scientific innovations which power the economy are generated from university research, society is beginning to be suspicious of the research outcomes. Innovations such as Genetically Modified (GM) foods are not widely accepted by the general population. People feel that they do not gain from enormous investments in research such as Artificial Intelligence (AI) and Genomic Biomedicine, which seem to only benefit tech giants or the very rich. There is a fear of what AI might bring, other than job replacements. Will we one day be ruled by a class of superhumans created by genomic research and controlled by AI robots?

Universities have a vital role to play in this "post-truth" society, yet their academic mission is increasingly under threat. How can university leaders protect academic integrity while navigating the current trend of commercialization? Who is best qualified to lead these institutions into the future: someone invested in teaching and research, or simply a good manager? How will universities contribute to public debates, dispelling the rise of "fake news"? From climate sceptics to anti-vaccination movements, anti-science rhetoric is being touted for political expediency. Universities are best placed to question and confront society's most complex and confounding problems, using scientific discovery to enable human progress. They must stand up to the array of anti-intellectual movements sprouting across the developed world, ensuring that assertions are backed up by evidence and not allowing public dialogue be hijacked by unsubstantiated claims.

CHAPTER 8

A Rapidly Changing Landscape

Abstract: Neoliberal reforms have resulted in educational consumerism. But recent labor market data shows that increasing the number of university graduates is not producing corresponding economic success. Many graduates now work in non-graduate jobs. Nevertheless, universities have expanded their global student markets as they see the growth of international students as a panacea for the decline in domestic students. But the reliance on a limitless flow of fee-paying international students cannot be maintained, as their home countries' universities are growing their own capacities.

Keywords: Apprenticeship, Educational Consumerism, Skill-Based and Work-Based Training.

At the beginning of the 21ˢᵗ century, most national government policies are predicated on the assumption that economic growth will be higher if a greater number of citizens receive a university education. This assumption has justified unrestrained university expansion in many countries – an unintended consequence of neoliberalization and the marketization of universities in late 20ᵗʰ century. However, labor market data shows otherwise: increasing the number of university graduates is not necessarily producing economic success. The growth in graduate jobs has not kept pace with the growth in the number of graduates. In fact, many graduates now work in non-graduate jobs. For many people, a degree is no longer automatically associated with earnings that are well above the non-graduate average. In reality, the modern labor market requires a more differentiated system (Wolf 2017). It is no longer true that university is the only really valuable option at tertiary level, and that any other sort of tertiary institution is simply second-best.

Businesses are now calling for more skill-based and work-based training, such as apprenticeship, where students can earn and learn at the same time. Yet governments have not been providing the necessary incentives and financial support for technical education; meanwhile, they heavily subsidize university enrolments. Businesses now appeal to universities to emulate the German model of close cooperation between universities and industry, where the typical University of Applied Sciences has mandatory practical internship and teaching staff who possess extensive industry experience. The focus in this model is on practice, and graduates from this system seem to have good employment outcomes. The UK Government is starting to invest in new institutes of technology as an alternative pathway for young people instead of asking the universities to work with existing technical colleges. The British Prime Minister was reported to express that it is "unwise to force less academic pupils into the straitjacket of university, leaving them drowning in debt for the sake of a poor degree -- particularly when we have a chronic shortage of British plumbers and engineers" (Else 2017).

The 21ˢᵗ century economy is an innovation-driven economy heightened by the digital revolution and global competition. These converging trends pose critical challenges for universities, who must meet the demands of new research and learning imperatives, respond to new forms of competition, and explore new modes of operation. The globalized economy and global expansion of the knowledge industry has eroded the monopolistic position previously enjoyed by universities. Advances in information and communication technologies are becoming critical as they transform teaching and learning, and fundamentally alter the way that universities deliver programs. Neoliberalism has been embraced by governments throughout the world to reform and reposition their national economies to respond to global competition. The resultant neoliberal reforms have corporatized the public sector – particularly universities, because of their potential economic contribution through development of human capital, research and innovation.

Neoliberal reforms have resulted in the educational consumerism. The rising costs of expanding higher education systems have outstripped national governments' capacity to pay, and governments are anxious to offload some of this cost burden. Besides allowing universities to charge tuition fees to domestic students, governments encourage their universities to expand into global student markets. Many Western governments have comprehensive strategies for recruiting international students, aiming to increase their market share and establish their national brand in the highly competitive international student market. Ambitious targets are set for attracting fee-paying international students. For instance, Australia aims to have 720,000 international students onshore annually by 2025, Canada wants to recruit 450,000 international students by 2022, and China aims for 500,000 international students by 2020 (British Council 2017). New Zealand wants to double its market share of international education by 2025, while Malaysia aims to attract at least 200,000 international students to its higher education institutions by 2020. Not to be outdone, the South Korean Government also has a national strategy to triple the country's international student number to 200,000 by 2030.

Even though the US and UK still command the lion's share of the global student market, the US's market share has slipped from 28% in 2011 to 22% in 2016, while UK market share remains stagnant at 11%. More than half of these international students are from Asia, which forms the largest group of international tertiary students. At the same time, there has been accelerating growth in education hubs in Singapore, Malaysia and Hong Kong and the establishment of international branch campuses in China, South-East Asia and the Middle East. We have witnessed the increasing capacity of Asian universities, and there has been a recent trend of Asian students preferring to study in the Asia-Pacific region.

The OECD's Education at a Glance 2017 (OECD 2017) reports a rapidly expanding tertiary-educated population worldwide as well as remarkable growth in global student mobility in the last two decades. It is projected that the total number of internationally mobile students will reach eight million by 2025 (OECD 2017). In just nine years between 2005 and 2013, the number of international students has increased by 50%.

Universities in the UK have the highest percentage of international students. Over a fifth of students in the UK are international: 14 % of the undergraduate and 38% of the postgraduate population (Universities UK 2017). Nevertheless, the latest data from the Universities and Colleges Admissions Service (UCAS) reveals a drop in EU and domestic enrolments in UK universities. An alarming report from the *Sunday Times* (Gilligan 2017) accuses many of UK's top universities of increasingly recruiting lucrative overseas students with lower qualifications. The report revealed that half of Russell Group universities had declining domestic student enrolments (a drop of 28% since 2008) amid an increasing number of applications. In the same period, the number of non-EU students (who pay fees which are three to four times higher) rose substantially (15%). The UK Department of Education has promised to monitor whether domestic students are facing discrimination.

Australia has the second highest proportion of international students, after the UK, at 20.7%. The latest education export data from the Australian Bureau of Statistics (ABS) estimates the export value of international students in Australia at AU$28.6 billion (US$22 billion) for 2016/17, representing a 16% increase over the previous year. International education is Australia's third largest export earner, contributing more than 130,000 jobs to the country. For the higher education sector, the year-on-year enrolment growth for 2016–2017 is 15%. In a comparative study on the factors driving international student enrolments in Australia, the presence of an offshore branch campus or transnational education collaboration was found to have the greatest influence in attracting international students to the home institution (Marshall 2018).

Many Western universities see the growth of international students as a panacea for the decline in domestic students. But international markets can be fickle, easily impacted by the changing economic and political climate. In 2017, the US saw a 7% decline in new international students and a flattening of total enrolments (Fishcher 2017). The sharpest drops came from markets in India, followed by Brazil and Saudi Arabia, possibly influenced by new US government policies. In the US, growth in Chinese international student numbers has also slowed, falling from double digits to around 7%. On the other hand, the number of international students in Canadian universities grew by 20% in 2016, albeit from a low base. Australia has also seen continuing growth in its international student market – the nation has greatly benefited from the recent boom in international students, which is likened to its mining boom at the turn of the century.

Even so, the goal of pursuing ever-increasing growth for universities is not sustainable. With the aging demographics of many developed countries, the number of school leavers is declining. For example, Singapore is facing a shrinking student population: fourteen schools and junior colleges will be merged by 2019 to keep school sizes viable. Furthermore, the reliance on a limitless flow of fee-paying international students cannot be maintained, as their home countries' universities are growing their own capacities (Strait Times, April 2017).

The OECD Education at a Glance 2017 reported that the growth in outbound mobility – foreign enrolment in tertiary education worldwide – began to flatten out noticeably from about 2010 onwards (OECD 2017). The sharp increase in foreign enrolments in recent decades was largely driven by the knowledge-based and innovation-driven economy when local education capacities were not able to fulfil growing demand. However, much of that demand has now been met with by the development of home country institutions, the expansion of transnational education by foreign providers, and the provision of online education. In his 2017 book, *The Australian Idea of a University*, Professor Glyn Davis, Vice Chancellor of the University of Melbourne, warned that disruptive market forces could result in an overhaul of the higher education landscape. With critics predicting that by 2070 there may only be ten global universities left, Davis argued that the only way for a public university to survive is through "experimentation, innovation and resilience" (Davis 2017).

CHAPTER 9

The Rising Power of China and Asia

Abstract: Universities in the West cannot afford to be complacent. They must look towards Asia to understand the future of universities. The meteoric rise of China's university rankings has established the country as a global higher education superpower. China has embarked on another ambitious plan to further strengthen its higher education system. The Double World-Class Project is aimed not only at creating world-class Chinese universities; it is part of a broader plan to build its impact and influence in the global higher education landscape. The dominance of the West is diminishing. China's scientific ambition is to be the global science powerhouse.

Keywords: Nature Index, STEM (Science, Technology, Engineering and Maths), Tertiary Enrolment Rate (TER), The Belt and Road Initiative.

In his 2012 BBC Reith Lecture, "Civil and Uncivil Societies", Professor Niall Ferguson cautioned that the biggest threat to Western civilisation is *complacency*. Professor Ferguson is one of the world's most renowned historians, as a Professor of History at Harvard, Senior Fellow at the Hoover Institution at Stanford, and a Senior Research Fellow at Jesus College, Oxford University. He believed that the West could not just ascribe the rise of Asia to its economic transformation; these countries have also transformed themselves politically. He also pointed to the degeneration of Western institutions and their decline in quality during the same period. Ferguson reasoned that it is the mindset that "we are fine, our schools are great, our legal systems are terrific and our political system is just fine" that is deluding us. It is this kind of self-congratulation and complacency which overstates performance and conceals declines (Ferguson 2012). Resting on 20ᵗʰ century laurels makes progress difficult.

Professor Keith Burnett, Vice-Chancellor of the University of Sheffield, has also said that to understand the future of universities, we must also look towards Asia. The West should take note of China's rising academic empire (Burnett 2018). The meteoric rise of China's university rankings has established the country as a global higher education superpower. In the Times Higher Education 2018 World University Ranking, there are two mainland Chinese universities in the world top 30 and seven mainland Chinese universities in the world top 200. Six universities

Christina Chow & Clement Leung

from Hong Kong also feature on the list. Overall, China has 63 institutions in the Times Higher Education 2018 Asia University Ranking (Times Higher Education 2018).

Since the implementation of the 211 and 985 Project universities two decades ago, China has embarked on another ambitious plan to further strengthen its higher education system. The Double World-Class Project is aimed not only at creating world-class Chinese universities; it is part of a broader plan to build its impact and influence in the global higher education landscape (Huang 2017). The Double World-Class's long-term plan includes developing 42 world-class universities as well as 456 world-class disciplines in 95 universities by the middle of the 21ˢᵗ century. However, the plan does not entail a significant growth in the number of public universities (which almost tripled from 1071 universities in 1999 to 2880 in 2017). This means that the Chinese Government is completely focused on building the excellence of its existing top-tier universities. While the plan may seem a little ambitious, it is very achievable so long as the pipeline of excellent students keeps growing. No doubt, China's central Ministry of Education has the will and the power to direct and strategically invest in the appropriate universities and disciplines.

It is worth noting that China is investing heavily in the science and engineering disciplines as well as medical science and agriculture, areas that will drive the growth of the Chinese economy. As for student destination countries, China has displaced Australia, France and Germany to become the third top student destination behind the US and UK. While China has been the largest source country of international students globally, with over half a million Chinese students studying overseas in 2016, that growth has slowed to 4% in 2016, from a high of 14%. The massive government investment in creating its own world-class universities means that China is changing from a traditional student source country to a preferred destination. It is the most popular study destination in Asia. According to China's Ministry of Education, almost half a million foreign students were studying in China in 2016, with half of them coming from countries in the One Belt, One Road corridors.

Global university rankings are still dominated by the US, but this dominance is no longer taken for granted. The number of US universities in the world's top 100 slipped from 58 in 2003 to 48 in 2017, while China's rankings have quickly ascended (Calderon 2017). This is a significant geopolitical shift in the global university landscape. As the rankings of Western universities in the US, UK, Canada, Germany, France and Spain have flagged, institutions in Asia have risen.

In the US, expenditure per student in higher education remains the highest in the world. The country also has the highest tertiary enrolment rate (TER) and the highest proportion of people going to university. It has the largest supply of graduates, particularly in the 55 to 64 age group; almost a third of all graduates in the world's major economies come from the US (Schleicher 2016). American universities have the highest expenditure in research and the largest endowments, reinforced by a culture of philanthropic donations to colleges.

But this US dominance is shifting. China is now producing more graduates each year than the US and Europe combined, with predictions that the number of young graduates (25 to 34 age group) in China will rise by a further 300% by 2030 (Schleicher 2016). While US students struggle with high fees and Europe faces a lack of investment its universities, China and other Asian countries have speared ahead. Chinese students are twice as likely to study STEM (Science, Technology, Engineering and Maths) subjects as their American counterparts. There are similar trends in India and other Asian nations. It is projected that by 2030, China and India could account for two-thirds of Science and Engineering graduates in major economies (Schleicher 2016). China and India recognise the impact of technological innovations on economic progress and prosperity. Their governments have made massive investments in higher education at lower production costs. The strategy allows them to leapfrog to the top, posing a real challenge for the West, especially with the competition for talent in the knowledge economy.

We witness a strong growth in the establishment of education hubs across Asia, notably in Malaysia, Qatar, Dubai, Singapore, Hong Kong and China. Historically, these have been the source countries sending students to Western universities. Now they are rapidly ramping up their domestic capacities, hosting a range of foreign university branches and integrating the best aspects of foreign universities into their higher education systems. They no longer favor a one-way traffic flow of students to the West. They want a deeper engagement with Western universities with mutual benefits, but on their own terms. Many of these countries have developed cohesive education policy with ambitious goals. Rising dynamic universities in Asia, particularly in China, Japan and South Korea, are making their way to the top of the league tables. They are developing research collaborations and academic exchanges with world-leading universities as equal partners (Benson & Griffith 2017). In the 2017 Academic Ranking of World Universities, Japan has three universities in the top 100, with another four in the top 200. Taiwan has two in the top 200.

In the 2017 Times Higher Education's Global University Employability Ranking, British universities have tumbled, while Asian universities (specifically those in China, Taiwan and South Korea) have made significant improvements (Jenvey

2017). China's two top-ranked universities, Peking (27th) and Tsinghua (30th), now outrank several elite universities in the US, UK, Australia, Canada, and Europe.

Western universities are starting to lose their allure and can no longer rely on international students as a rich source of income. Asian countries are working hard to reverse the trend of outbound students. Through specially designed education hubs, they hope to attract a flow of international students from within the region as well as the West. The aim of many of these hubs is to integrate knowledge generation and innovation. Their goal is to create a critical hub of talents and expertise by encouraging foreign universities and R&D companies to establish a local base. For example, Singapore has attracted a number of leading foreign universities including University of Chicago's Booth Graduate School of Business, Duke University's School of Medicine, Yale University, MIT, and Imperial College to form partnerships with local universities. In doing so, it hopes to attract even more international students, academics and researchers from all over the world to make Singapore a global talent hub (Lee 2018). The US-based Cross-Border Education Research Team (C-BERT 2017) database had a total of 247 International Branch Campuses (IBC) in operation in 2017. From 2006 to 2010, the number of IBCs grew 45%; since 2010, it has grown another 26%. There are currently 22 more IBCs under development, suggesting ongoing growth.

China is also continuing to grow its soft power internationally, including investment in its Chinese cultural centres at universities worldwide. The Confucius Institute has a presence on all continents, in more than three-quarters of the world's countries (Orr 2017). China is using the charm of its culture and values to enhance its influence. Furthermore, China's One Belt One Road Initiative aims to integrate six Silk Road corridors into a cohesive economic region – a 21ˢᵗ century version of the maritime silk road – through capacity-building in infrastructure, cultural exchange and the broadening of trade. China has established a university alliance based at X'ian Jiaotong University which supports the Belt and Road Initiative. The University Alliance of the Silk Road aims to build educational collaboration and promote economic growth in countries along the Silk Road corridors. It was founded in 2015 and has more than 132 member universities from 32 countries in five continents. Its stated purpose is to support education, research, cross-cultural understanding and to foster cooperative education and international higher learning.

Through government leadership, China plans to triple its funding for basic research by 2020, raising it from 5% to 10% or US$ 34.5 billion. Research will be at the heart of the Chinese Government's future plan and it plans to invest 2.5% of its GDP into science research. It also wants to promote collaboration between universities and research centres in order to build a critical mass and create synergy between institutions. The aim is to enable a stream of breakthrough innovations which have real-world applications (Fei, Shobert & Wong 2016). The Chinese Government's commitment to scientific research is firmly grounded in the belief that science is the driver of innovation and economic growth, and that science will solve the big societal and environmental problems. China's scientific ambition is to be the global science powerhouse, and its investment in key technologies is overwhelming. It has conducted some of the biggest experiments and made ground-breaking medical advances. It has pushed the boundaries of exploration from the ocean depths to outer space. It has built the world's largest radio telescope, which aims to pick up radio waves from the far reaches of the cosmos, including ancient hydrogen signals, with a view to better understanding the evolution of the cosmos. The telescope detected two pulsars during its trial run in October 2017, and will continue the search for new stars and extraterrestrial life.

Other examples of China's scientific breakthroughs include the new cornea transplantation procedure developed by China Regenerative Medicine International (CRMI) based in Shenzhen. The procedure uses decellularized pig corneas as the collagen scaffolding for repopulating the recipient's own cells, thus avoiding tissue rejection. In 2017, China's scientists were the first to report the results of using CRISPR (a gene editing technique) in correcting genetic mutations in viable human embryos (Tang *et al.* 2017, Le Page 2017). In January 2018, researchers at the Chinese Academy of Sciences Institute of Neuroscience in Shanghai reported success in creating two identical long-tailed macaques through the cloning of non-embryonic cells. This marks the first time that primates have been cloned from a process called somatic cell nuclear transfer (SCNT). The process involves transferring the nucleus of a somatic cell with its DNA into an egg which has had its DNA already removed (Liu *et al.* 2018).

As a result of its huge investment and sheer effort, China continues to increase its global share of research publication. It now ranks second after USA in its contribution, based on the Nature index. In 2017, China published 11,136 articles in physical sciences, life sciences, earth and environmental sciences, compared to USA's 25,537, Germany's 9,092, France's 5,345, UK's 8,146, Canada's 3032, and Australia's 2,660 (Nature Index 2018). More than half of China's high-quality research involves international co-authors. China is trying to use science and technology to move away from its economic reliance on conventional manufacturing. According to the World Intellectual Property Organisation (2017), China has filed 1,204,981 international patents, compared to USA's 520,877, in 2016. The Nature Index also showed that China's cutting-edge life science and technology has boomed in Shenzhen and Beijing. Shenzhen has been transformed into a research-based industry hub, with companies in Shenzhen accounting for almost half of the nation's international patent filings. In 2016, ZTE Corporation was ranked number one with 4,123 patents, followed by Huawei Technologies with 3,692 patents. In comparison, in 2016, Hewlett Packard filed 2,466 patents, Intel 1,692, Microsoft 1,528, Google 584 and Apple 450 (World Intellectual Property Organisation 2017). Shenzhen's Beijing Genomics Institute (BGI) is not only the world's largest centre for cloning pigs; it is also the world's largest centre for gene sequencing. BGI has ambitions to sequence the genomes of a million people, a million animals and a million plants as well as the microbiome of the human digestive system (Shukman 2014).

China is investing heavily in medical research as its population ages. The country is already the world's second largest pharmaceutical market. It is advancing rapidly in innovative and personalized medicines and its innovation expenditure is expected to reach $1 trillion by 2020. It has a strong supply of talent with over 50,000 students graduating from its medical schools each year (Zhang & Zhou 2017). Joseph Jimenez, CEO of Novartis AG, wrote in the World Economic Forum that "There's a research revolution going on in China – and one day it could save your life" (Jimenez 2016). Based on UNESCO data and the World Economic Forum Human Capital index, China had 4.666 million recent STEM graduates in 2016, while India had 2.575 million and the US had 0.568 million. Chinese STEM graduates outnumber US STEM graduates 8.2 to 1. This ratio will increase with the number of Chinese young graduates rising by a further 300% by 2030. By contrast, Europe and the United States will see modest growth of around 30%. By 2030, China and India could account for more than 60% of the G20 nations' workforce with a STEM qualification (OECD 2015). It is predicted that Europe and the US will lag behind at 8% and 4% respectively. By 2030, China is projected to have fifteen times more STEM graduates than United States (Schleicher 2016).

CHAPTER 10

The Omnipresent Threat of Disruption

Abstract: So far, universities have been able to avoid disruptive innovation. Instead, they have grown bigger and better, albeit by charging high tuition fees and incurring hefty student debts. Now, with local student demand flattening and graduate employability declining, some universities find themselves in financial stress. Escalating tuition, rising student debts, the unbundling of higher education services and the rapid advance of learning technologies mean that higher education is ripe for disruption. In their race to expand and pursue ranking excellence, universities have driven up costs and lost focus on their academic mission. They are now unsustainably over-extended, and unaffordable for most of the population. The commodification of higher education in the last century has made universities more vulnerable to disruptive competition.

Keywords: Academic Mission, Commodification of Higher Education, Disruptive Innovation, Learning Styles, Multiple Intelligences, Technological Core.

In the last few decades, even the most successful businesses have to face the challenges of disruption and radical change. So far, universities have been able to avoid disruptive innovation. Instead, they have grown bigger and better, albeit by charging high tuition fees and incurring hefty student debts. Now, with local student demand flattening and graduate employability declining, some universities find themselves in severe financial stress. So, in this climate of customer unaffordability and public disillusionment, are universities ripe for disruption? How relevant are the brick-and-mortar universities with the rise of MOOCs?

Harvard Business School's Professor Clayton Christensen, speaking at the Colgate University Symposium on Innovation and Disruption in Higher Education, expressed a great concern over the future of universities (Christensen 2014). He predicted that half of the colleges and universities in the US could go bankrupt in 10 to 15 years. In their race to expand and pursue ranking excellence, universities have driven up costs and lost focus on their academic mission. They are now unsustainably over-extended, and unaffordable for most of the population.

The truth is that the commodification of higher education in the last century has made universities more vulnerable to disruptive competition. Historically, traditional universities have had no serious competition, other than emulation by new entrants (Christensen 2011). Their academic mission was complex and their business models were not for making a profit. The prestige and esteem of the traditional universities were held in high regard for their scholarship, discoveries and pursuit of knowledge for its sake. New entrants could only replicate the success of the incumbents by emulating the academic culture – a culture which has been enriched by communities of scholars in perpetuating the tradition of knowledge creation, accumulation, preservation and dissemination. Now that universities have been marketized, the quality of their products, mostly undergraduate and postgraduate taught programs, are commodified. The measure of teaching quality is reduced to student satisfaction surveys, quality control, and performance measures, which can be replicated. Escalating tuition, rising student debts, the unbundling of higher education services and the rapid advance of learning technologies mean that higher education is ripe for disruption. Disruptive competitors, from private providers offering online degrees to companies running their own corporate universities, have become a formidable competitive force that threatens traditional universities. These competitors will be able to engage a larger, underserved segment of the higher education markets.

Disruptive innovation, a term coined by Professor Christensen, defines a process by which a disruptive product innovation or service establishes itself initially in simple applications at the bottom end of the market, then unrelentingly makes its way towards the upper end of the market, eventually displacing the established incumbents. Historically, disruption in business models has been the dominant mechanism for making things more affordable and accessible. Professor Christensen cites numerous examples, including the disruption of minicomputers by personal computers, integrated steel mills by minimills, vacuum tubes by transistors, Ford by Toyota, Mercedes by Lexus, Xerox by Canon, IBM by Microsoft, Sony Diskman by Apple iPod.

In disruptive innovation, new entrants typically enter at the bottom end of the market, selling simple and affordable products to consumers who could not otherwise afford more sophisticated existing products. At this stage, the incumbents who dominate the market with better high-end products would not consider the low-end product as a threat. It is a strategy that works well for new entrants. In his book, The Innovator's Dilemma: When New Technologies Cause Great Firms to Fail (Christensen 1997), Professor Christensen examined the downfall of successful and seemingly unassailable companies. He identifies the cause as those competitors coming from the lower end of the market, who make products affordable to new segments of customers.

The strategy of new entrants sneaking in at the low end of the market is very effective. One does not kill a giant by fighting it head on. By attacking at the bottom end of the market, which the incumbent may have little interest in dominating, the new entrant can get a foothold and bide time to improve its products. This is the reason why successful companies find it so hard to stay at the top, since there is no obvious sense in defending low profit markets. But the lesson here is that purely pursuing profit can lead to the demise of institutions. Professor Christensen cites other examples: Toyota Corona targeted the bottom of the market, since dominant players tend to ignore products with a low profit margin. Toyota became a leading player, but it has since been disrupted by Korean-made cars such as Kia and Hyundai, which have taken over the low end of Toyota's market. The phenomenon of disruptive innovation is important to a country's economic growth. For example, in the 1990s, Japan's economy took a dip. The engine of Japan's macroeconomic miracle in 1970s was due to entrants like Toyota, Honda, Sony, Canon, Mitsui, and Seiko disrupting dominant players in the US. As a result, many of the US's large companies shrank and eventually died. Fortunately, the US continues to create new companies and new industries with venture capitals (Japan does not have a venture capital culture or labor market mobility). Japan has since been disrupted by Korea, Taiwan, Singapore, Hong Kong, China and India. Macroeconomic prosperity depends on the ability to continuously disrupt. Yet this disruption model does not work well for some service industries, such as hotels. Hotels do not have a technological core which can be extended, except through emulations; hence, the hotel business cannot be disrupted with lower cost and better products (Christensen 2011). But in the case of higher education, online learning has changed the game remarkably. Online learning brings to higher education a technological core that can enter at the lower end of the market and be extended upwards.

Another factor in disruptive innovation identified by Professor Christensen relates to competition against non-consumption. As companies develop innovations, they tend to innovate products faster than the needs of their customers, thinking they can charge higher prices and get a better profit margin. As a result, many companies end up having products that are too expensive and sophisticated for their customers. In so doing, they unwittingly invite disruptive innovation into the low end of the market since the dominant players would not regard these disruptive innovations as killer competitors as they focus only on the high profitability products. In the beginning, these disruptive innovations typically serve a completely new segment of consumers, who cannot afford sophisticated, high-end products. At first, disruptive innovations tend to have lower gross margins and simpler products that do not attract the attention of the incumbents. But as these new products improve, they pull customers from the incumbents (Christensen 2011).

Professor Christensen fears that this is what is happening to high education. In the past few decades, some of the traditional universities have grown bigger and better, as exemplified by Harvard University. In the book The Innovative University: Changing the DNA of Higher Education from the Inside Out (Christensen & Eyring 2011), the authors write extensively on the history of Harvard. Harvard had humble beginnings as a small liberal arts college, with associated professional schools that admitted students without a college degree. It bore little resemblance to today's modern research university. However, beginning in the 1870s, three towering presidents, Charles Eliot, Lawrence Lowell, and James Conant, engineered its institutional DNA to transform it into the great university we know today. Eliot's dictum of "everything at its best" in Harvard has meant that it has the best scholars, the best research, the best students, the best range of subjects and the best facilities. But Harvard's idea of "the best" is becoming increasingly expensive. Without the financial strength of a Harvard, universities following this model would struggle to become "the best". Harvard has managed to sustain its model as "the best" due to its prodigious fundraising capabilities, amassing an endowment of $35.7 billion in 2017. For other universities, the strategy of emulation can work for a while, with economic growth resulting from the massification of higher education. However, as the costs of running a comprehensive research university climb, the escalation in tuition fees becomes unaffordable for many students. Professor Christensen warns, "Historically, higher education has avoided competitive disruption. One reason for this past immunity is the power of prestige in the higher education marketplace, where the quality of the product is hard to measure. Now with more focus on outcomes and the steady improvement of low-cost online learning technology, the prospect of competitive disruption is real" (Christensen & Eyring 2011).

For centuries, universities had no "technological core" and were bound by their physical locations, thereby making disruption impossible. However, in the 21ˢᵗ century, that obstacle has been removed. Course content can be captured by low-cost technology for distribution *via* livestream and podcasts; learning management systems can be made available 24/7 to students anywhere in the world. While universities have been using online content for the last two decades, this is not considered a form of disruption as it is only used as a form of delivery, not a new business model, according to Professor Christensen (Christensen 2014). Rather, online content is a kind of sustaining innovation which merely improves existing delivery. Many universities use online learning, but they accommodate it as part of the existing rigid, teacher-centric curricula.

Until now, university curricula have been based on proprietary and interdependent architectures, since individual universities have their own organizational and academic structures to deliver their idea of the best learning. But these architectures are very expensive to customize. Online learning making customization easier, to suit learners' styles, capabilities and needs. Currently, in an effort at cost-cutting, many universities are discontinuing low enrolment non-core courses, particularly those in the humanities. When these courses are axed, it presents an opportunity for online learning to ensure that these important subjects persist beyond financial trends.

Moreover, real learning is hindered by traditional modes of one-size-fits-all teaching, which may not be motivating for some groups of students. Instead, the organization of subject content should be aligned with the learner's specific intelligence and aptitude. The theory of multiple intelligences was proposed by Howard Gardner of Harvard. His work in psychology and human cognition led to the identification of ten areas of intelligence: verbal-linguistic, logical-mathematical, spatial-visual, kinaesthetic, musical, interpersonal, intrapersonal, naturalist, existential and moral intelligence (Gardner 1993). Addressing the multiple intelligences of learners can help universities customize their teaching effectively. Professor Christensen believes that computer-based, learner-centric, on-demand learning will disrupt teacher-led classes. In time, online education will be enhanced by machine learning, artificial intelligence, virtual reality and other emerging technologies. People in professional development, adult education, and remedial learning, as well as students in developing countries, could benefit from customized learner-centric education.

As MOOCs continue to improve, they allow more competitors to enter at the bottom of the market. Online courses are more flexible and modular; students can take any course for shorter duration at a fraction of the cost, without being tied to a rigid academic program. Continuous innovations have enhanced the online learning experience; these include high-quality, low-cost videoconferencing, and virtual experience which allow students to work in groups in virtual international laboratories or manage global projects using computer simulations. New generation learning management systems allow customization of the curriculum, giving students just-in-time learning tools. Through the use of these technologies, students can elect the best model that suits their learning and life style. Artificial intelligence can serve as a virtual teaching assistant, providing tutoring and personalized learning and reducing the need for instructor contact. Learning analytics can help students learn more effectively. Studies have shown that the use of these technologies provides comparable learning outcomes for students with fewer hours of study. Blockchain technology is now being used to record grades and qualifications which are fraud-proof.

The current metrics for measuring university performance focus on faculty qualifications, publications, High Citation index and Impact factor, university ranking, and graduate employability. However, in online learning, measurements are focused on teaching alone. Professor Christensen cites his experience with the University of Phoenix, an online university in US where he was invited to record his ten best lectures. The production of the lectures was stage-managed. The theatre was filled with attractive models to brighten up the lectures. These model actors exhibited various facial expressions in response to the lecture content. At moments when the students' attention might wander, the camera would pan to the audience, showing the model students absorbed in the lecture. These lecture clips were professionally edited with animated 3D Powerpoint. The University of Phoenix invests 200 million each year in improving their teaching, and teaching is all they focus on. The number of students currently enrolled in their MBA is around 135,000 (compared to 900 at Harvard Business School).

The incumbent universities are currently protected by government regulation, accreditation, and academisation. New entrants would have to work around regulation and network effects to compete against non-consumption. There is a rigid academic architecture in most universities with interdependencies between disciplines making customisation very difficult. Not only teachers are not able to customise, the rigid model of learning can demotivate some students. On the other hand, online learning is easier to customise as they are modular. Currently, most research universities are integrated vertically conducting both research and teaching. However, it is questionable if the research is informing the undergraduate curriculum. Now that knowledge is in abundance, modularity could be made possible. Without the need for co-ordination of the interdependent courses, modularization and standardization would drive administrative cost down. Once online learning becomes modular, innovations can be easily adopted which could scale up very quickly. But in an interdependent architecture system, it is hard to adopt innovations and harder still for innovations to diffuse and be accepted at universities.

This theory of disruption may well apply to those universities that operate purely as a business, commodifying learning, offering credentials, delivering content, and focussing on margin, profit and growth but without pursuing the true academic missions. But, as stressed by Professor Christensen, the key to the inimitable competitive advantage of universities are held by the truly inspiring faculty with their expertise and ability to inspire students. It is unfortunate that many universities regard their faculty purely as a means of production in a knowledge economy.

Importantly, we need to examine what is the intrinsic value of a university education. Is it the intrinsic nature and value for its own sake as distinct from the value for something else to which it leads? Most of the time, we tend to promote mainly the extrinsic values derived from a university education such as personal and economic benefits. And this has led to a tendency to exaggerate the potential benefits of a university education by university marketers. Perhaps we should promote the intrinsic value of a university education to give students more realistic expectations. Universities are not simply about the delivery of content, which is fast becoming ubiquitous. Have the neoliberalization, marketization and commodification of university education led to the demise of genuine learning? When universities promote customer first, they set up expectations for students to expect a quality service for which they demand satisfaction and fulfilment of promise – a job. What is the inimitable essence of a university education? It should have economic, social and cultural impact beyond immediate job prospects. How do we survive this disruptive transition? It is not enough just to develop online teaching: we need a different model to serve the needs of our students and society.

CHAPTER 11

A Reason to Survive

Abstract: What is the unifying thread of this centuries-old institution? How university as an institution which has undergone so many transitions through the centuries still remain strong as a higher learning institution? Throughout this narrative, the purpose has been to search for the quintessence of the idea of a university, the core principle which has enabled it to endure. One of the more coherent concepts is that of "understanding". In this context, "understanding" encompasses a broader concept – from enquiry, critical debate, self-understanding, self-discovery, self-reflection and self-knowledge to the pursuit of truth. As such, "understanding" has the ability to bind all those who believe in the search for truth and in the idea of a university, to be believers through the quest for knowledge.

Keywords: Self-Discovery, Self-Knowledge, Self-Reflection, Self-Understanding, The Idea of a University, Truth-Seeking.

The birth of the modern university has its origins in the Middle Ages and the Enlightenment (Delanty 2001). The production and elaboration of knowledge was seen as a means of achieving social progress. Protected by academic autonomy and freedom, the university played an important role in bringing about social change. Its progress in sciences and technologies gave the university influence and power with business and governments. This modern university had a unity of purpose to pursue excellence.

The 1970s saw the beginning of the end of this model of the modern university. Universities became increasingly subject to the expectations and aspirations of prevailing political, cultural and social values, as well as labor market demands (Sabour 2005). In this period of late modernity, governments began to view universities as sources of highly specific benefits and marketable commodities. They came to assume that the main function of the university was to be the provision of direct benefits to economic prosperity, innovation and national wealth (Boulton & Lucas 2008). In making these assumptions, governments ignored the fact that such benefits are only by-products of the deeper and more traditional functions of a university. It is feared that governmental focus on universities as purely economic instruments will ultimately undermine the university's contribution to society.

In the final decades of the 20th century, universities have been subjected to multiple pressures from governments to improve their performance in exchange for public support. As a result, universities have become more like corporations and have difficulty in clearly defining their missions (Barnet 2000; Jarvis 2001). They have taken on various forms according to the fashion of the time, such as the entrepreneurial, innovative or performative university. They are expected to generate not only intellectual but economic capital. For example, the European Commission stipulates that the education, research and innovation agenda for its universities must include increasing research productivity and research-based innovation and technology, providing curricula to meet labor market demand, securing diversified funding, and supporting regional development (European Commission 2006).

What is the unifying thread of this centuries-old institution? How university as an institution which has undergone so many transitions through the centuries still remain strong as a higher learning institution? Throughout this narrative, the purpose has been to search for the quintessence of the idea of a university, the core principle which has enabled it to endure. One of the more coherent concepts is proposed by Barnett (2011), who believes that the "unifying idea" of a university is that of "understanding". In this context, "understanding" encompasses a broader concept – from enquiry, critical debate, self-understanding, self-discovery, self-reflection and self-knowledge to the pursuit of truth. As such, "understanding" has the ability to bind all those who believe in the search for truth and in the idea of a university, to be believers through the quest for knowledge. Moreover, Barnett (2011) asserts that the concept of self-understanding is essential for any individual, organization or society who wishes to become enlightened. As Professor Barney Glover, Chair of Universities Australia, has said, "The core objectives universities pursue can never be about any other agenda than the truth" (Glover 2017).

The idea that university is constituted on the fundamental principle of self-knowledge and self-discovery can be applied to the development of individuals. Based on this universal principle, the modern university supports its students in their self-discovery and their engagement and interaction with the world (Simons 2007). Moreover, as institutions of higher learning, universities teach and research in order to gain a better understanding of self and the world, including finding solutions for global problems. The idea of truth-seeking and understanding is particularly relevant in the 21ˢᵗ century, a postmodern era in which information seems to be equated with knowledge and where evidence, intellectual inquiry and expertise are under sustained attack. Knowledge and understanding have the ability to refine the character of the student, broaden and cultivate the intellect. In an age of mass production of degrees and diplomas, it is essential to examine what university education really means and supposes to do. The emphasis of a true university should be on the improvement of the mind and the understanding of truth.

Arguably, this is a rather abstract concept, but it need not conflict with the performance measurements instigated by national governments. An out-and-out obsession with metrics to the exclusion of the education of the mind could leave universities vulnerable to the fickleness of the market when environments change and metrics fall. The improvement of the mind and the understanding of truth should be the overarching principle of a university. The identification of a raison d'être enables the university to adapt and respond to changing circumstances without sacrificing its unrivalled distinctiveness. It also makes it easier to explain to the state and society what a university is for. In modern management parlance, it is a core competency which is hard to replace, raising the barrier to entry in Porter's competitive five forces model. In turn, this central principle gives rise to the concept of self-governance, autonomy, and freedom of expression.

In the 21ˢᵗ century, the postmodern university seems to have lost its sense of self-enquiry. It has ignored self-understanding and the critical debate of itself, necessary conditions for the growth of the individual and the organisation, society and the country. This intellectual approach should be one of the university's distinguishing attributes. In his address to the National Association of College and University Business Officers in July 2014, Bill Gates (Lederman & Rivard in Inside Higher Education 2014) questioned why universities are not good at examining themselves even though their academics are good at studying the world. He warned that universities must hold themselves more accountable, otherwise someone else will do the job for them.

When universities struggle to produce graduates with employable skills, it becomes clear that university education should be about more than cosmetic and vocational trappings, measured by graduate earnings. It is not enough for universities to focus solely on job-specific skills in this rapidly changing world, where content is quickly made obsolete. How does the pursuit of knowledge address the skill gaps facing our society? The aim should be to equip students to learn how to think and improve their understanding of themselves and the world. If students only grasp narrow, discipline-specific knowledge, we are only producing workers for the industrial society of the 20ᵗʰ century.

In the 21ˢᵗ century and beyond, we need people who can think and imagine, synthesizing new knowledge across disciplines: minds which can continuously innovate and be master of machines. In a society which fears being ruled by machines and algorithms, should we not stop and ask who should be controlling the algorithms of artificial intelligence? If algorithms claim to know us better than we know ourselves – as in the case of Google, Facebook, Amazon, and the many Apple apps which try to tell us what we are like – shouldn't we want to get ahead of those algorithms, and know ourselves better? We should vehemently maintain control of technology and not allow technology to rule us. This is what university education should be about: learning how to think inventively, coming up with ground-breaking ideas, finding out how to respond to complex challenges and unpredictable circumstances.

How do students gain such capabilities? They need more than specialized knowledge: they need exposure to literature, philosophy, and history in order to shape their world views and exposure to the sciences so that they can understand how technologies work. How often do we encounter people whose mindsets merely reflect their narrow professional training? What we need is engineers who can understand the biological perspective, and computer scientists who can comprehend philosophy and emotional intelligence. That is where future innovations will come from: the interface between machine and humanity.

Faced with the current crisis in universities, where institutions churn out large number of underemployed graduates, students should be given a solid grounding in wide areas of studies for a well-rounded education. We need a balance of specialization and general education. This helps students build the kind of resilience, civic responsibility and moral commitment which will serve them well in all future endeavors.

Let's face it: university is not for everyone. Access does not mean that everyone should go to university. National government policies are predicated on the incorrect assumption that economic growth will be higher if a greater number of citizens have university education. With this belief, they turned universities into a system of further education – like an extension of high school – rather than higher education. In turn, universities have oversold the idea that a degree is the only guarantor of future success. They have created a generation of unfulfilled graduates, and now this promise has come back to haunt them.

The erosion of confidence in universities is a sign that current university leaders have failed to explain the public value of universities to society. The university has a much greater role than simply granting qualifications and giving out diplomas. Its most important function is that of shaping the whole individual. Cardinal Newman's notion that "a university's 'soul' lies in the mark it leaves on students" may prove useful guidance, as crucial decisions are made about the future of our universities (Deboick 2010).

CHAPTER 12

Leadership in a VUCA World

Abstract: This chapter looks at the concept of a VUCA (Volatile, Uncertain, Complex and Ambiguous) environment brought on by politics, society, economy and the environment. To counter uncertainty and ambiguity in this environment, internal organizational simplicity is needed to enable an institution to be agile and responsive. It requires a different focus on strategy and leadership development – one which focuses on vision, understanding, clarity, and agility.

Keywords: Adaptive Thinking, Agility, Complex and Ambiguous, Complexity, Uncertain, Volatile.

The concept of VUCA (Volatile, Uncertain, Complex and Ambiguous) was first introduced in the early 90s by the US Army War College to describe the increasingly multilateral world which emerged after the end of the Cold War (Kinsinger & Walch 2012), but it was not until the events of 9/11 that the term actually took hold (Lawrence 2013). The term VUCA has subsequently been adopted in strategic management to describe the chaotic, turbulent, and rapidly changing business environment that has become the new norm. The concept became more popular after the Global Financial Crisis of 2008 as the world witnessed companies collapsing, business models rendered obsolete, technological disruptions, the explosion of social media, and global disasters. The concept is especially pertinent when it comes to the development of leadership, since leaders' skills are becoming obsolete with their organisations subject to the VUCA landscape. VUCA reflects the constantly changing challenges brought on by politics, society, economy and the environment. This environment requires a different focus on strategy and leadership development – one which focuses on vision, understanding, clarity, and agility.

VUCA has been driven by increasing digitization, connectivity, trade liberalization, global competition, and business model innovation, which all converge to make environments highly unstable and unpredictable. The increasing number of players in a globalized world contributes to the complexity, since cause and effect cannot easily be identified. Increasing complexity makes it difficult to understand both threats and opportunities. To counter uncertainty and ambiguity in this environment, internal organizational simplicity is needed to enable an institution to be agile and responsive. This is particularly important in the case of universities, where there has been an explosion in administrative staff and costs. As a result, universities have become more like dinosaurs: too big and heavy to shift quickly.

We have been conditioned by decades of teaching to think that the world is predictable. Now we must deal with a future in which change continually grows in speed, nature and magnitude, with possibilities increasing exponentially. In this context leaders have to focus on what is possible rather than on what is probable. They need to possess more complex and adaptive thinking, and the ability to take on multiple perspectives. They must make continuous shifts in people, processes, technology, and structure in order to respond to the new environment. Leaders today have to process huge amount of information and make faster decisions in an interconnected world. Instead of planning to reduce uncertainty and problem-solving, astute leaders turn uncertainty into opportunity – but this requires a high level of agility (Kail 2010 & 2011; Kavanaugh, & Strecker 2012).

CHAPTER 13

The Fourth Industrial Revolution

Abstract: This chapter looks at the current Fourth Industrial Revolution which integrates the basic sciences and technologies of physics, chemistry and biology, blurring the boundaries between the physical, digital, and biological worlds. The convergence of these technologies has created unprecedented breakthroughs - computations and algorithms based on the process of evolution are now applied in creating artificial intelligence and in genetic programming to simulate artificial neural networks. Advanced technologies will perform at a level higher than human experts in terms of accuracy and output. They will also revolutionise multiple industry sectors simultaneously. As such, the disruption of work practices and displacement of human workers occur at a much faster speed than in the past. Hence, the Fourth Industrial Revolution will make university-level education even more vital.

Keywords: Advanced robotics and autonomous transport, Artificial intelligence, Automation, Disruption, Fourth Industrial Revolution, High-level machine intelligence (HLMI), Lifelong learning, Machine-learning, MOOCs, Skills gaps and skill mismatch.

Society has experienced waves of profound technological change, with resultant growth in productivity and prosperity. The first two industrial revolutions largely involved the use of newfound energy sources, such as coal, electricity and petroleum, which allowed human energy input to reduce. The third industrial revolution harnessed the power of electronics and digital technology to automate and scale up production. The current Fourth Industrial Revolution integrates the basic sciences and technologies of physics, chemistry and biology, blurring the boundaries between the physical, digital, and biological worlds. The convergence of these technologies has created unprecedented breakthroughs. For instance, computations and algorithms based on the process of evolution are now applied in creating artificial intelligence and in genetic programming to simulate artificial neural networks. Other technological breakthroughs include cell-sized robotic implants which stimulate tissue growth and the use of machine learning to synthesize new biomaterials and help find cancer cures.

The speed of these technological advances in the Fourth Industrial Revolution are growing exponentially in velocity, scope and impact, disrupting almost every industry sector in every country. Its impact and transformation affects the entire value chain and systems of current production, management and governance, which were largely based on the Second Industrial Revolution (Schwab 2016). These old management practices were designed to be linear and mechanistic, following a strict "top down" approach which is now obsolete in the new business models. Advanced technologies will perform at a level higher than human experts in terms of accuracy and output. They will also revolutionise multiple industry sectors simultaneously. Hence, the disruption of work practices and displacement of human workers occur at a much faster speed than in the past.

Automation will displace a significant proportion of work worldwide. According to McKinsey Global Institute's research (MGI 2017), half of all work activities could be automated with current technologies such as artificial intelligence and robotics within the next ten years. Although few occupations would be completely automated, around 60 percent of occupations could have 30 percent of their activities fully automated. This means that the future of work will need substantial workplace transformations. McKinsey's scenario planning suggests that by 2030, as much as 14 percent of the global workforce will need to change their occupational classifications. Workers will need to adapt and learn alongside intelligent machines. Such adaptation requires a high level of education. Workers will also need soft skills such as creativity and cognitive, social, emotional capabilities, which are more difficult to automate.

While the current industrial revolution and automation will displace workers and cause job losses, it can also create new jobs and opportunities. Based on McKinsey Global Institute's research, there are seven trends which will contribute to future labor demand. These are: rising consumer incomes; investment in education; the aging population and a consequent demand for better healthcare; investment in renewable energy and energy efficiency; technology development and deployment; infrastructure investment; and marketization or shifting of unpaid housework and childcare to paid employment to enable more women to take part in the workforce. Job growth should occur in healthcare, for doctors, nurses and allied health professionals. Other job growth areas should include education professionals at all levels, scientists, researchers, computer specialists, engineers, designers, management and construction workers as well as artists and entertainers. By the same token, the jobs most susceptible to automation would be those carried out in predictable settings which could be translated into logarithms.

The outcomes of these seven trends vary significantly from country to country, depending on factors such as demand, wage, demographics and other economic factors. Occupations in job growth areas tend to require high levels of education and advanced training. While the nature of jobs may evolve, future work activities are predicted to require a more adaptive approach in terms of application of expertise, interaction with teams, and problem-solving. This means that workers will need to possess social, emotional and cultural intelligence; creative and innovative thinking; cognitive skills; and logical and lateral thinking.

LIFELONG LEARNING

The concept of lifelong learning is a practical way to help workers adapt and update their knowledge and skills continuously, in order to operate effectively in unstable environments. This kind of continuous learning can enhance an individual's employability and career advancement. Consequently, the Fourth Industrial Revolution will make university-level education even more vital. The availability of e-learning would allow workers to self-pace, learning skills flexibly with interactive learning resources at a time convenient for them. Open Educational Resources or MOOCs (Massive Open Online Courses) offered by many world-class universities are available, either for free or at extremely low cost. Universities have a crucial opportunity to form partnerships with industry in training the future workforce and helping them transition to new jobs. This will be a viable model for businesses to scale up the training of their staff without incurring the high costs of internal training.

CHAPTER 14

Future-Proofing University Graduates

Abstract: This chapter looks at the time horizon when AI would outperform humans in activities. Yet there are serious skills gaps and mismatch exist in many national economies. It is evident that there is an imbalance between the skills produced by the higher education system and the adoption of technology by businesses. Due to the unprecedented rate of change in current technological trends, it has been estimated that nearly 50% of subject knowledge acquired during the first year of a technical degree could be outdated by the time students graduate. This means that, in addition to technical and specific knowledge, students need to acquire stable core skills which are resistant to change and difficult for AI to program. These core skills relate to human characteristics such as judgment, abstraction, empathy, critical thinking, optimism, entrepreneurialism, cultural intelligence, association and system thinking: all essential abilities relevant across industry sectors.

Keywords: Abstraction, Association and System Thinking, Cognitive Abilities, Critical Thinking, Cultural Intelligence, Empathy, Entrepreneurialism, High-Level Machine Intelligence (HLMI), Judgment, Optimism, Skills Gaps and Skill Mismatch.

Researchers from Oxford and Yale Universities have recently completed a large survey, investigating machine-learning researchers about their predictions on the development of artificial intelligence (AI). Specifically, the researchers were asked to estimate when "high-level machine intelligence" (HLMI) could be achieved – *i.e.*, unaided machines would be able to perform every task better and more cheaply than human workers. Based on current trends, the researchers projected that AI would outperform humans in a number of activities in the next 10 to 35 years. They believed that there would be a 50% chance that AI would outperform humans in all tasks in 45 years and automate all human jobs in 120 years (Grace *et al.* 2017). However, there was wide variation in subject response. Asian respondents expected AI to achieve HLMI in 30 years, while North Americans expected it to take place in 74 years. The huge disparity may have something to do with China's recent announcement of its goal of achieving AI world leadership by 2030 (McDonald 2017).

The survey found that AI would outperform humans in activities such as language translation by 2024; driving trucks by 2027; working in retail by 2031; writing a bestselling book by 2049; performing a surgical operation by 2053; and conducting AI research by 2102. Advances in AI have an immense societal impact. For example, autonomous self-driving technology may replace millions of driving jobs in the coming decade, leading to massive unemployment around the world. This would have numerous implications for current laws and regulations, regarding the infrastructure and cyber-security of such a transport system. The researchers' estimates are important, as they will enable policymakers to prepare for trends in AI and attempt to minimize their potential risk.

THE SKILLS GAP

There are serious skills gaps and skill mismatch in many national economies. Skill shortages significantly impact the ability of companies to grow and compete. One reason for the shortage is the growing disconnect between businesses and higher education – but this is not a perception shared by universities.

According to a 2015 Gallup poll (Busteed 2015), only 11% of business leaders regarded university graduates to be work-ready, even though university academic leaders believed that their students were adequately prepared for work. Moreover, only 35% of surveyed students believed that they were prepared for work. A McGraw-Hill Education 2016 Workforce Readiness Survey again found that only 40% of students believed universities and colleges prepared them for work. Brandon Busteed, Executive Director of Education and Workforce Development at Gallup, said that if universities were the auto industry, they would be forced to recall a quarter of all their graduates.

Research by OECD (Quintini 2011) has shown that the qualification mismatch is widespread in many OECD countries. As many as one in four workers are over-qualified, while one in three are under-qualified for their jobs. Underutilized skills and skill deficits have important consequences on job satisfaction and turnover. Studies on skill mismatch conducted in Australia and the United Kingdom found that graduates in the humanities are more likely to be over-qualified than others, while skills deficiencies are significantly more likely for high-tech jobs. Many analysts believe that the rapid upsurge in the number of university graduates relative to demand could be one of the causes for qualification mismatch (Bessen 2014). There is a delicate balance between the skills produced by the higher education system and the adoption of technology by businesses.

One of the world's largest business organizations, the US Chamber of Commerce Foundation, has joined force with USA Funds, a US global equity investor, to explore strategies to address the growing skills gap facing US businesses. Through the Chamber's Center for Education and Workforce, a Talent Pipeline

Management initiative has been established, which gives employers a stronger role in communicating the positions and capabilities they require. US employers have long been frustrated by the rigid college accreditation system, which they believe is a barrier to innovation. Instead, they argue for an alternative, employer-driven approach to recognize and certify talent. They want to be part of upskilling and developing their current workforce, as well as inducting new graduates into industry. A new model of university-employer collaboration would work on demand planning and forecasts, and make known the competencies and credential requirements for critical positions which are driving the skills gap. University leaders need to face the reality that the most common reasons for students to complete a degree are to find a good job and to be competitive in the workforce, to provide financial security and life fulfillment. As such, university leaders need to work closely with employers to improve students' employment prospects.

Due to the unprecedented rate of change in current technological trends, it has been estimated that nearly 50% of subject knowledge acquired during the first year of a technical degree could be outdated by the time students graduate (World Economic Forum 2016). This is due to the current technological trends which are causing an unprecedented rate of change in the core curriculum content of many academic fields. A focus on the current state of the workforce pipeline for traditional formal qualifications and 'hard skills' therefore risks understating the scale of impending skill disruption, if a significant part of the existing subject knowledge of the current workforce will largely be outdated in a few years. It is projected that on average, by 2020, more than a third of the desired core skill sets of many occupations will comprise of skills that are not yet fully known nor considered crucial to today's jobs. The main technological drivers for this speed of change are mobile internet and cloud technology; advances in computing power and big data; new energy supplies and technologies; the Internet of Things; advanced robotics and autonomous transport; AI and machine-learning; advanced manufacturing and additive printing; and biotechnology and genomics. In fact, it is predicted that most of the existing subject knowledge of the current workforce could be outdated in just a few years (World Economic Forum 2016).

This means that, in addition to technical and specific knowledge, students need to acquire stable core skills which are resistant to change and difficult for AI to program. These core skills relate to human characteristics such as judgment, abstraction, empathy, critical thinking, optimism, entrepreneurialism, cultural intelligence, association and system thinking: all essential abilities relevant across industry sectors. The World Economic Forum (2016) recommends a core set of 35 work-relevant skills and abilities:

• Cognitive abilities (cognitive flexibility, creativity, logical reasoning, problem

sensitivity, mathematical reasoning and visualisation)
- Physical abilities (strength, manual dexterity and precision)
- Basic skills including active learning, oral, reading and written skills, ICT literacy, and processing skills (active listening, critical thinking, monitoring of self and others)
- Cross-functional social skills including emotional intelligence, negotiation, persuasion, service orientation, training, and teaching
- Systems skills including judgment, decision-making and systems analysis
- Complex problem-solving skills
- Resource management skills (financial and material resources, people management and time management)
- Technical skills (equipment, programming, quality control, technology design)

It is predicted that children entering schools today will eventually end up working in jobs that have not been created yet. New technological trends will create many new cross-functional roles where employees will need both technical and social/analytical skills to survive (World Economic Forum 2016). However, many universities continue the 20ᵗʰ century tradition of providing highly specialized training in narrow disciplines. This model of education needs to change. University leaders should work closely with businesses and national governments to imagine the curriculum needs of the 21ˢᵗ century. To prevent unwelcome surprises, leaders need to monitor global trends and undertake technology forecasting.

CHAPTER 15

Preparing Students for Complexity and Change – A Liberal Education

Abstract: This chapter looks at how a liberal arts and science education can prepare students for complexity and constant change. It cites examples to illustrate the importance of studying humanities. Humanities teach students critical thinking and help students to become adaptable, to learn and think independently. To prepare students for a successful career they need to develop the intellectual and emotional intelligence to cope with uncertainty and ambiguity. When students are exposed to liberal arts, they are likely to become more self-aware and self-disciplined, acquiring virtues such as empathy, compassion, resilience, and courage.

Keywords: Communication, Duke Kunshan University, Global Awareness, Harvard Liberal Arts Education, Hong Kong, Humanities. Intellectual and Emotional Intelligence, Liberal Arts and Science Education, Melbourne Model, Miami Global Plan, Singapore University of Technology and Design, Sydney University.

In recent decades, liberal arts and science education in the United States has come under criticism for lacking economic utility. As higher education in the country suffers a crisis in confidence, declining public support and a new push for the tangible value of knowledge, the reputation of liberal education has suffered. There is a widespread misconception that a liberal arts degree focuses only on the humanities. In fact, most liberal arts programs include components of basic sciences. They offer precisely the soft skills that employers find lacking in current graduates. While it faces criticism in the US, liberal arts education is increasingly embraced by other countries including China, Hong Kong, and Australia. It is believed that in the age of AI, humans need to learn skills which cannot be replaced by algorithms: creativity, empathy, adaptability, collaboration, emotional and cultural intelligence, critical thinking, entrepreneurialism.

The value of a liberal arts education has been argued most convincingly by the President of Miami University, Dr Gregory Crawford. Crawford is himself a physicist by training, but has found that a liberal arts education, particularly in the humanities, gives him a different perspective on life (Carter 2016). Miami University initiated a model in which humanities and science can complement each other. Crawford believes that humanities ground students in the kind of moral values needed for leadership. Humanities also teach students critical thinking and help students to become adaptable, to learn and think independently. What today's students need for a successful career is the intellectual and emotional intelligence to cope with uncertainty and ambiguity. When students are exposed to liberal arts, they are likely to become more self-aware and self-disciplined, acquiring virtues such as empathy, compassion, resilience, and courage.

In addition to learning their professional disciplines, the Miami University model, known as the Global Miami Plan, helps students to learn from the liberal arts, including communication, writing and analytical skills as well as global awareness. The Miami Plan consists of a liberal arts core in addition to the professional disciplines, covering English writing, fine arts, humanities, social sciences, world cultures, and the natural sciences including biology, physics, mathematics, formal reasoning, and technology. Thus, whatever they choose to study, students learn from both the humanities and basic sciences and receive a breadth of knowledge. They also learn how to develop the practical critical thinking skills involved in problem-solving: examining evidence and pros and cons, developing arguments and counter-arguments; comprehending the underlying assumptions of multiple perspectives; and drawing solid conclusions after examining all sides of an issue or problem. They learn how to contextualize analysis and explore political, social, economic and historical or other contexts which surround the problems or issues. Crucially, they learn how to work effectively in group settings: how to listen actively to the ideas of others and how to negotiate a shared understanding of complex issues and tasks. The Global Miami Plan encourages students to both reflect and act on their new knowledge. Students also learn about decision-making on complex intellectual and ethical issues, such as how to be a global citizen. The aim of the program is to train future leaders. Miami University is among the universities producing the greatest number of Fortune 500 corporate leaders in the US.

Similarly, the Harvard liberal arts education provides a broad-based education in the social sciences, natural sciences and the humanities, as well as depth and concentration in a particular academic field of specialization. The program aims to provide the foundational education for developing students' intellectual capacity rather than catering for vocational preparation. This general education helps students to orient themselves in the world, and empower them to imagine the lives they wish to lead. Liberal education exposes students to complexity, contradiction, and ambiguity, and then use the knowledge they have acquired to solve problems (Reuben 2015).

In Australia, the University of Melbourne adopted a form of liberal education called the Melbourne Model in 2008. This liberal education model aims to help students to be critical thinkers with the flexible mindset required to solve future problems. It offers a suite of undergraduate programs which support specialist knowledge as well as academic breadth. In China, there has been a growth in the introduction of liberal arts and sciences programs to local universities as well as the new joint ventures between Chinese and Western universities. For instance, Duke Kunshan University, a joint venture between Duke and Wuhan Universities in partnership with the city of Kunshan, offers an interdisciplinary, integrated liberal arts and sciences curriculum with problem-based and team-based learning. The program aims to prepare lifelong learners with a sense of social responsibility, imbued with purpose and passion. Duke Kunshan University seeks to use its innovative pedagogies to serve as a platform for higher education innovation for China, the US, and the world. At a time of critical debate about the direction of higher education, the University hopes that its experiments in liberal arts and science education in China will provide significant lessons for the West (Godwin & Pickus 2017).

Hong Kong also introduced a General Education curriculum to its higher education system in 2012. The aim was to strike a new balance between breadth and depth which transcends specialization. For example, the University of Hong Kong's four-year General Education program consists of common core courses in combination with disciplinary majors, minors and electives, incorporating a diverse range of subject and learning experiences. The focus of the program is on whole-person education, arousing students' intellectual curiosity, and an emphasis on experiential and service learning in an environment rich with culture.

Another example relates to the Singapore University of Technology and Design (a joint venture with Massachusetts Institute of Technology) whose education model is based on combining the fundamentals of mathematics, science, and technology and the humanities in arts and social sciences. It uses design as a focus to develop an integrated multi-disciplinary curriculum and unique educational programmes in architecture, engineering and information technology.

Instead of yet another honours program, Australia's Sydney University is offering students a special four-year program known as the Bachelor of Advanced Studies. This gives students an extra year in which to acquire lifelong work skills which will enhance employability. It acknowledges that employers are looking for graduates who not only possess technical knowledge but are agile, able to work with people from other cultures, and have the smarts to apply their skills to real-world problems outside the classroom. The University is offering courses to help students to develop key skills such as inventiveness, cross-cultural competency, project management, ethical leadership, data science and coding. The students can mix and match according to their preferences and create their own expert niche. They may participate in special research projects, industry work experience, or in community projects.

It is not sufficient to be educated only in scientific skills – one must learn about social and historical contexts to understand how science works in the broader world, as well as knowing how to communicate the value of science. We need more interaction between science and humanities. The dichotomy between arts and sciences has not been conducive to nurturing talent and producing future leaders. Therefore university leaders should seriously reimagine what kind of curriculum is needed to equip students for the 21ˢᵗ century.

CHAPTER 16

Back to Teaching Basics

Abstract: This chapter looks at the neglect on teaching by universities as a result of the research ranking exercises which consume a great deal of universities' energy at the expense of their teaching. Now, with declining student satisfaction and deteriorating student outcomes, national governments are starting to turn their attention towards the teaching mission of universities. In an attempt to refocus universities' efforts on teaching, a Teaching Excellence Framework (TEF) was developed by the UK Government to recognize and reward excellence in teaching and learning, and also help inform prospective student choices in higher education. The chapter also examines the concept of Active Learning, and the benefits of neuroscience research to enhance student learning.

Keywords: Active Learning, Cognition, Memory, Multitasking, Neural Resources, Neurogenesis, Neuroplasticity, Neuroscience, Student-Centred Educational Model, Teaching Excellence Framework (TEF).

In the past few decades, national governments have introduced research performance assessments in order to determine resource allocation at a time of declining budgets. This kind of assessment began in the United Kingdom in 1986, and involved ranking research universities' outputs in a number of fields. However, these research ranking exercises not only resulted in the closure of academic departments, they currently consume a great deal of the energy of university leaders and staff, at the expense of the universities' teaching. Now, with declining student satisfaction and deteriorating student outcomes in completion and employability, national governments are starting to turn their attention towards the teaching mission of universities.

In an attempt to refocus universities' efforts on teaching, a Teaching Excellence Framework (TEF) was developed by the UK Department for Education to recognize and reward excellence in teaching and learning, and also help inform prospective student choices in higher education. However, participation in TEF is voluntary: individual universities can decide whether or not to take part.

Successful participants in the TEF assessment receive a gold, silver or bronze award reflecting their standards of teaching, learning environments and student outcomes. Universities are assessed on a range of measures including student satisfaction, drop-out rates and whether students go on to employment or further study after graduating. The exercise only covers undergraduate teaching. The assessment is conducted by an independent panel who take into account differences between institutions, such as entry qualifications and subjects studied, when determining the final awards (Pells 2017). A gold award means that the university is of the highest quality in the UK, with outstanding teaching and excellent student outcomes. The silver award is for universities exceeding national requirements, and the bronze is for those who meet the national requirements. To incentivize universities to refocus their efforts on teaching, all universities given a bronze award or higher will be able to increase their tuition fees in line with inflation in 2018/19.

A total of 295 UK Higher Education providers took part in the Teaching Excellence Framework in 2017. In the assessment, 59 providers were rated gold, 116 were rated silver and 56 were rated bronze. Interestingly, only eight of the 21 Russell Group universities which took part were given a gold rating. Russell Group universities are perceived to be the best in the country, but even some world-renowned universities received comparatively low ratings. In fact, many of the traditional universities were outperformed by newer universities.

Student performance relates to student engagement with their learning (OECD 2016). Although some factors associated with high levels of attrition are beyond the control of institutions (family and financial pressures, poor preparation), universities can assist in managing student expectations and clearly communicating to students what is expected of them in terms of personal effort and assessment requirements. The use of tutorials to help students understand complex issues and the strategic use of predictive analytics followed up with proactive counselling are effective strategies.

THE SCIENCE OF LEARNING: ACTIVE LEARNING

Professor Carl Weiman, the US Nobel Laureate and physicist and educational theorist at Stanford, has stated that one of the biggest problems facing universities is the lack of systemic process for measuring teaching quality and learning effectiveness. He argues that university administrators are too obsessed with publishing and research funding. Since faculty are not rewarded for high-quality teaching, they focus their efforts on research output in order to pursue tenure and academic promotion while neglecting teaching (Westervelt 2016). Professor Weiman has spent a good part of his career measuring the effectiveness of lectures versus scientific methods of teaching. He uses a "clicker" electronic device to record students' responses to his lectures and finds that students generally retain only 10% of what they are taught in lectures.

Wieman is convinced that big undergraduate lectures are ineffective and overdue for a reform. Instead, he is in favor of getting students to learn actively by solving problems. In his introductory quantum mechanics courses at Stanford, he uses the flipped classroom model by giving students some pre-reading which he follows with a mini-lecture. He then assigns a problem for students to discuss and solve in small groups. During these discussion sessions, he walks around the classroom, listening in or helping out when students are stuck. As such, Wieman sees himself as a cognitive coach. His lectures only serve to prime students for grappling with complex concepts. He does not want students to learn passively from lectures; he prefers to stimulate their minds by challenging and monitoring what they have learned. Wieman has scientifically measured the performance of these active learning methods over pure lectures, and has been able to demonstrate a substantial drop in failure rates and increase in test scores. He argues that the data powerfully demonstrates the superiority of active learning, believing it is almost unethical to teach otherwise. He believes that the biggest obstacle to universities adopting new methods of learning is the reward system of tenure, which is tilted towards research productivity and funding, with little regard for the effectiveness of undergraduate teaching.

Major advances in cognitive psychology and brain research have advanced the science of learning. One of the primary goals of learning is to achieve expert thinking. Research has found that the explicit practice of expert thinking, paired with timely and specific feedback, facilitates effective learning. Active learning increases students' understanding in science, engineering, and mathematics (STEM). Results of controlled studies comparing conventional teaching with scientifically informed methods of teaching find that the scientific approach results in dramatically improved test scores, with students learning six times as much.

Instead of passive listening, the active learning approach requires students to do tasks or interactive simulations. They have to explain how they come up with their problem-solving strategies. By using new simulative technology, students are able to learn highly complex concepts at a much earlier stage of their university programs (Wieman 2015 & 2017). This model of active learning has been trialled in some universities, including the University of Colorado Boulder and the University of British Columbia in Vancouver. With so much academic content now available freely on the internet, the role of universities in providing content should be questioned. Rather than just asking students to memorize theories and facts, universities should help students learn and think about the knowledge they have acquired.

NEUROSCIENCE RESEARCH

Neuroscience research has found that structured learning, standardized assessments and stressful learning environments do not promote positive learning in students (Kaufer 2011). In neurobiological terms, learning involves changing the brain. While moderate stress is beneficial for learning, mild or extreme stress (as measured by the level of cortisol) is detrimental to learning. Active learning stimulates multiple neural connections in the brain and promotes memory. For optimal learning to occur, the brain needs to be able to change in response to stimuli (neuroplasticity) and produce new neurons (neurogenesis) (Kaufer 2011). The most effective learning occurs when multiple regions of the brain are engaged in the learning task: the regions associated with memory, the senses, higher levels of cognitive functioning, and the desire to learn.

A student-centred educational model should encourage this deeper, superior learning by ensuring that classroom experiences are relevant to students' lives and interests. Other factors which contribute to optimal learning are innovative content, engaging instruction, blended learning, multimedia resources, interactive technologies such as virtual and augmented reality, work-integrated learning, and learning support. Recent neuroscience research also demonstrates that multitasking in a learning environment results in lower performance (Ellis, Daniels & Jauregui 2010). Dual-tasking drains neural resources and can result in memory degradation and compromise recall. This might prompt universities to teach subjects in blocks, instead of having four or five subjects run concurrently over a semester. Focused attention in an environment that encourages single matter concentration appears to be the most powerful factor in learning uptake. Back-to-back scheduling reduces students' cognitive capacities towards the end of the day as students need space and rest to consolidate their learning. The job of the inspiring teacher is to seize the students' attention and direct their thinking towards an active learning experience (McCandliss 2015). Truly effective teaching changes cognition and leads to the rewiring of the brain.

CHAPTER 17

Listening to Our Students

Abstract: Universities in the 21ˢᵗ century have to pay more attention to the needs of students and help students understand the best intention of universities in facilitating their learning journey. They have to provide students with value for money and tangible outcomes. They have to be mindful of students' wellbeing.

Keywords: Learning Facilities, Student Academic Experience Survey, Student Finance, Student Support Services, Student Wellbeing, Teacher Access, Teaching Hours.

The old practice of universities setting the rules expecting students to willingly follow is no longer working. The modern university have to listen to its students and provide the outcomes that they need. Student outcomes might include the learning experience, skills and knowledge acquisition, wellbeing, industry experience, time taken to complete a degree, graduation rates, value for money, employment opportunities, earning potential, community contributions and life satisfaction. Some of these outcomes are difficult to quantify and depend on the timing of the measurements. Students who found certain subjects difficult may subsequently realize their critical importance, later in their careers. Such outcomes will not be captured by instant student surveys. The challenge is to help students understand the best intention of universities in facilitating their learning journey.

Student well-being has recently become a focus as students come under more financial pressures, struggling between academic workload and part-time jobs. Escalating tuition fees is a continuing concern raised by students around the world. The results of the 2017 UK Student Academic Experience Survey (Neves & Hillman 2017) found a continuing decline in students' perceptions of universities' value for money. The number of students who perceived their university education as poor value (34%) was only slightly less than the number of those who perceived it as good value (35%). In Australia, the government's 2017 Graduate Outcomes Survey National Report discovered that between 2008 and 2017, the proportion of graduates who were reluctantly underemployed had increased by 10.8% to 19.7%. More than a quarter of students reported that their degrees were not relevant to their jobs.

On the subject of value for money, the UK survey revealed that an overwhelming majority of students (74%) did not believe that they received adequate information on how their fees were spent. Only 25% of students felt that their experience had been better than expected, a decline from 27% in 2016. Furthermore, 13% of the students thought their experience had been worse than expected. A lack of support from or connection to academic staff was cited as the primary reason for the less-than-expected experience. One-third of the students reported that they would have chosen another course if given a second chance. Overall, 65% of students thought that they had learned a lot, 27% said that they learned a little, while 7% reported not learning much.

There is an obvious link between access to staff and perceived value. On the whole, the UK survey showed that students greatly valued their contact with teachers. They generally believed that teaching staff were helpful and supportive, and worked hard to make subject matter interesting. However, the students felt that still more could be done to improve their learning experience. For example, they would like teachers to help them explore their own areas of interest and initiate debates and discussions. Moreover, they would like the teaching staff to motivate them to do their best. This level of personal contact would require smaller class sizes. However, there is an obvious trade-off between high volumes of contact hours and class sizes. Only 20% of students said that they had sufficient access to academic staff outside class hours. The survey revealed that students did not regard being a leading and active researcher as an important quality in a teacher, contrary to what most universities espouse. Students preferred staff with professional expertise, who continuously developed their teaching skills.

Student wellbeing has come to the fore in recent years. At both undergraduate and postgraduate levels, the survey showed declines of 2-3% in all four measures of wellbeing: life satisfaction, feeling of life worth, happiness, and anxiety. However, the first three measures seem to correlate with the degree to which students feel they are learning. That is, students who felt that they learned a lot reported more positive levels of fulfilment. This indicates the importance of a productive learning experience to wellbeing.

When it came to university budgets, students were nearly unanimous that expenditure should not be cut back on teaching hours, student support services, student finance, and learning facilities. They would rather see a reduction in spending on campus building and sports facilities – they do not want to study on a construction site (Neves & Hillman 2017).

CHAPTER 18

Tensions between Teaching and Research

Abstract: This chapter looks at the cross-subsidies between teaching and research to cover shortfalls in research funding, and the close link between student fees and research productivity in universities.

Keywords: Cross-Subsidies, High Profit Margins Courses, Oversupply of Graduates, Productivity Commission, Research Funding, Research Productivity, Teaching-Only Staff.

In Australia, a close link between student fees and research productivity in universities has been identified by Norton & Cherastidtham (2015). In particular, the data showed that high international student fees correlated with the number of research publications by each university and their Excellence in Research Australia (ERA) ranking. Norton & Cherastidtham (2015) were able to demonstrate that universities with high fees produced the most number of publications and were associated with high-quality research output. The resultant higher rankings were viewed by students as a measure of prestige, and this has a significant influence on the level of fees the universities could command. The authors concluded that international students were willing to pay a substantial premium in order to attend prestigious, highly-ranked universities. The revenue surplus generated by these high fees allows universities to cross-subsidize research; on average, Australian universities allocate 20% of their teaching surpluses to support research activity. However, the authors believed that this formula would not be sustainable and would negatively impact the quality of university teaching. Indeed, Australian universities are reporting decreasing student satisfaction as well as larger class sizes.

The Australian Productivity Commission's 2017 Report on University Education, *Shifting the Dial: 5 Year Productivity Review* (Commonwealth of Australia 2017), highlights the tensions between universities' research and teaching functions. The report likened the relationship between research and teaching to favoring the golden child over the forgotten progeny. University staff are far more likely to be rewarded for research performance than for teaching. Around 80% of teaching-only staff were in casual roles in 2015, compared to less than 8% for research-only positions. Most of the casual academic staff were employed at the tutor level, and were themselves students studying towards a doctorate. They lacked teaching experience and skills, and generally did not have a teaching career as a goal. Teaching quality clearly plays second fiddle to research, with consequences for student satisfaction and graduate outcomes. This is not surprising, given that global university ranking systems are all heavily tilted towards research performance, with only a small weighting (10 – 30%) given to teaching. Universities do rely on their rankings to attract international students.

The Australian Productivity Commission Report pointed out that while *average* student outcome indicators remain acceptable, the metrics mask serious issues. In the last decade, the full-time employment rate for recent graduates has been falling consistently, from 85.2% in 2008 to 70.9% in 2016: a low not seen since the massification of higher education in Australia. The underemployment ratio for graduates was 20.5 % in 2016, compared to around 9% in the general economy. Many graduates are employed in roles unrelated to their studies, indicating that their degrees have contributed little value. To address this problem, the report recommends that consumer law be applied to universities in Australia, as is done in the United Kingdom. Moreover, a significant number of employers are unhappy with the graduates they have hired; in the 2016 Employer Satisfaction Survey, around one in six business supervisors said they were unlikely to consider hiring another graduate from the same university.

Universities would be well-advised to better align their incentives to the interests of students and taxpayers. Their obsessive focus on research has led them to channel the profits made from teaching to cross-subsidize research. It has been found that universities tend to accept more students in programs with high profit margins, which are cheap to teach but command high fees; the result is an oversupply of graduates in disciplines such as Law. By the same token, universities restrict intake into programs which are expensive to teach, meaning that there is a dangerous shortage of graduates in vital areas such health, science and engineering.

While it is understandable that universities, like other economic agents, respond to market and profit incentives, should they be for forgiven for acting largely on financial motives? Shouldn't they be held accountable for failing in their academic missions? When university leaders fail to understand their institutional missions, market incentives begin to dominate.

In a university's academic mission, research and teaching do go hand in hand. However, university leaders tend to use the teaching-research nexus as the rationale for justifying cross-subsidies from teaching to research, in the pursuit of research rankings. The Productivity Commission Report argued that studies in Australia and overseas had found little evidence to support a positive relationship between teaching outcomes and research capabilities.

The failure of the universities to perform their teaching duties has led to the Productivity Commission endorsing the Australian Government's performance-based approach to funding based on student outcomes. Surely this is not a good outcome for universities, since institutional autonomy is a critical part of their foundation. Nevertheless, universities have brought this on themselves by pursuing profit over academic mission.

In British universities, there is a similar situation where research is underfunded and the shortfall is made up through tuition fees (Olive 2017). More than a quarter of research activity is unfunded, and teaching surpluses were needed to finance 14% of all UK university research in 2014/15. One of the main problems is that research funders increasingly seek matching funding to maximize their investments, with little regard for the long-term consequences for universities. Olive's 2017 report, *How much is too much? Cross-subsidies from teaching to research in British Universities*, warns that UK research cannot continue to be funded on such unsustainable principles, becoming a "race to the bottom" rather "than a race to the top". The report calls for a sustainable business model which neither exploits students nor jeopardizes research.

The UK is a top research performer, with twelve institutions listed in the top 100 universities in the 2018 Times Higher Education World Rankings, and three in top 10. However, a substantial portion of its research is unfunded and has to be made up from non-publicly-funded teaching surpluses, mostly from international student fees and other commercial incomes. There is a funding gap of at least £1 billion that needs to be filled to make research sustainable. On average, each international (non-European) student contributes over £8,000 to UK research. In coming years, this income cannot be guaranteed, with declining international student enrolment numbers. At the same time, the UK Government has put a freeze on domestic tuition fees at £9,250, putting further pressure on universities to cover the costs of teaching across the board. And then there is Brexit. Universities UK reports that EU research funding, which account for £1.86 billion of output, is at risk (Kelly 2016).

Olive (2017) offers some solutions: undoubtedly the best of these is for the UK Government to boost research funding without increasing the volume of research. Based on OECD 2015 data on public investment in research, the UK is below the OECD average of 0.65% at 0.46% of GDP. This is in comparison to Korea's 1%,

Finland's 0.84%, Germany's 0.83%, France's 0.77%, and the US's 0.67%. Keeping the current budget but reducing the volume of research would make research more sustainable. However, this would require a change in strategic direction: either reducing the number of universities conducting research or reducing the range of research areas. It is worthwhile to note that UK research is already concentrated in the twenty-four Russell Group universities which receive three-quarters of research incomes.

This is a strategy which should also be considered in Australia. Reducing the range of research areas should be within the purview of individual universities, according to their strengths. Continuing cross-subsidies to cover shortfalls in research funding is simply not sustainable. The argument that research necessarily informs teaching is not well-founded, since there has been little evidence that this cross-fertilisation benefits students. More than ever, students are demanding better value for their investment.

CHAPTER 19

The Impact of Research

Abstract: National governments are increasingly encouraging universities to focus more strongly on research impact: on the contribution that research makes to society, economy, health, and the environment, and not just its contribution to academia. An example of research impact is the control of the Ebola epidemic in West Africa. The outbreak of Ebola was successfully conquered with the combined efforts of university, charitable foundation, industry and regulator.

Keywords: Avian Flu, Clinical Trial, Ebola Epidemic, Pandemics, Vaccines.

National governments invest billions in university research because they believe excellent research and new ideas are fundamental to economic progress. Until recently, most research assessment has emphasized on the quality and output of the research. But governments are increasingly encouraging universities to focus more strongly on research impact: on the contribution that research makes to society, economy, health, and the environment, and not just its contribution to academia.

One shiny example of research impact is the control of the Ebola epidemic in West Africa, one of the poorest parts of the world. Before its sudden outbreak in 2014, there were no drugs nor vaccines available for this deadly virus, which has the highest case fatality rate (70%) known to medicine. According to the World Health Organization, during the 2014-15 Ebola outbreak, a total of 28,616 cases were reported in Guinea, Liberia and Sierra Leone, with 11,310 deaths. While vaccines are the most effective way to control infectious diseases like Ebola, there was no commercial business case to make the vaccine, as it would be hugely expensive and could take years.

However, through the concerted efforts of Oxford University's Jenner Institute (renowned for its expertise in vaccine research), the US Vaccine Research Center, the North American Biodefence, the US Army Medical Research Institute of Infectious Diseases, the National Institutes of Health (NIH), and the Public Health Agency of Canada, three candidate vaccines were developed in months, as opposed to years, in late 2014.

After the candidate Adenovirus vaccine was successfully tested in animals to be 100% effective, a tiger team was formed comprising the World Health Organization, Welcome Trust, GlaxoSmithKline, OKairos (a biopharmaceutical company spun out from Merck), Johnson & Johnson, and NIH Plan and Regulators to undertake the Phase I clinical trial in human volunteers with the view to conducting a Phase III trial by December 2014. This was an amazing and unparalleled turnaround time to get a candidate vaccine to trial. In the end, Merck and Co, GlaxoSmithKline and Johnson & Johnson produced three candidate vaccines for human clinical trials. A novel vaccine for Ebola was thus developed in just nine months, overcoming the regulatory, funding and logistics hurdles. An innovative trial design was also successfully implemented from Phase I leapfrogging to Phase III, skipping Phase II clinical trial altogether. The outbreak of Ebola was successfully conquered with such incredible R & D efforts (Hill 2016).

This is a remarkable case of research impact. The outbreak of Ebola was successfully conquered with the combined efforts of university, charitable foundation, industry and regulator. The lesson from this case is that the world needs to have outbreak preparedness to guard against dangerous viruses such as Influenza, Zika, MERS (Middle East Respiratory Syndrome), Rift Valley Fever, Hendra, Lassa, SARS, and West Nile. Of particular importance is the threat of the next flu pandemic - the bird flu or avian flu caused by a sub-type of influenza viruses - H7N9. During a recent outbreak, 88% of people infected contracted pneumonia, three-quarters ended up in intensive care with severe respiratory problems, and 41% ultimately died of the infection. The world urgently needs to guard against future pandemics, and university research – whether or not a commercial argument exists for conducting it – will play a vital role in our preparedness.

From correcting genetic errors with molecular scissors (CRISPR) to treating leukemia with personalised gene therapies (CAR-T cell immunotherapy); from discovering earlier human origin (about 300,000 years ago) to tracking nutrient changes in crops due to climate change; from observing the astronomical event of head-on collision between two neutron stars to finding seven Earth-sized exoplanets, universities are critical in advancing the global research impact.

CHAPTER 20

Collaboration with Industry

Abstract: Close collaboration with industries is key to university success. There is a trend of bringing industry to university campus to enhance student employability and technology transfer. The chapter cites many examples including: the Boeing Advanced Research Center on the University of Washington's Seattle campus, IBM's Research and Development Laboratory at the Melbourne campus, Microsoft's global Station Q quantum at the University of Sydney, and Siemens' Industry 4.0 "Factory of the Future" Swinburne's Melbourne campus.

Keywords: Brain Belts, Open Innovation, Rust Belts.

Industry collaboration is key to the sustainability of universities. The current trend of bringing industries to university campuses is an excellent way of enhancing student employability and addressing workforce solutions. Co-location of university and industry is a very useful model which brings real-world learning into classrooms and produces work-ready graduates. The close collaboration enhances technology transfer, industrial partnerships, student internships and work-integrated learning. Co-location facilitates spontaneous interactions between staff and students and overcomes the physical barrier between industry and academia. It gives students the opportunity to learn from professionals and potential employers, in order to understand industry's real needs and acquire hands-on professional skills such as teamwork, project management, and interpersonal and communication skills. Industry, on the other hand, can benefit from the technology transfer, keeping abreast of the latest research. They will also have the opportunity to influence and improve the education of future workers.

There are many examples which demonstrate the successful collaboration between companies and universities. The Data Science Laboratory at Ludwig-Maximilians University in Munich is an excellent example of the close collaboration between industry and academia. The Laboratory brings together students, researchers and professionals under one roof to work on data analytics and artificial intelligence.

At the University of Washington, Boeing has built a Boeing Advanced Research

Center on the university's Seattle campus. The laboratory allows the company to work side by side with students and faculty on the challenges of the industry, such as the design and structure of aircraft and spacecraft. Not only does the close collaboration enhance Boeing's basic and applied research and translational R&D, it will ensure that the university's students have the skills needed to become the next generation of aerospace leaders. In 2017, Boeing opened a new advanced development research centre at Georgia Institute of Technology's campus in Atlanta. The Boeing Manufacturing Development Center enables Boeing researchers and Georgia Tech engineering students to co-operate to help drive the development of innovative factory automation in aerospace engineering, and to solve some of the toughest technical challenges in aircraft manufacturing. In Australia, the University of Queensland has become the first university to co-locate with Boeing in the Asia-Pacific region. A team of Boeing engineers from Boeing Research & Technology has moved from the company's Brisbane headquarters to the University's engineering research hub at the St Lucia campus. Boeing Australia has the company's largest R&D presence outside the US. At the Boeing Research & Technology Centre, Boeing will work with other university partners and Small and Medium-sized Enterprises to conduct R&D work on aviation technology, unmanned aerial vehicles, automation, aircraft systems, modelling and simulation.

Another example involves IBM and its close collaboration with Australia's University of Melbourne. In 2011, IBM opened a new Research and Development Laboratory at the Melbourne campus. The co-location of the laboratory with the university provides enhanced skills training for undergraduate and postgraduate students and researchers. The Laboratory focuses on three key areas: natural resource management, disaster management, and healthcare and life sciences. The latter involves the translation of life science research into clinical applications including neuroscience, protein science and structural biology. Furthermore, in December 2017, the University, a leader in quantum computing, joined IBM as a founding member of the IBM Q Network Hub to pursue the development of quantum computing technology. The Network is a global partnership involving leading Fortune 500 companies, universities and national research laboratories to explore quantum applications for business and science with commercial, intellectual and societal benefits. The IBM Q Network will serve as a platform to make quantum computing more accessible to businesses and organisations through access to the most advanced IBM Q systems and quantum ecosystem. The hub will provide users access to the Q system in order to run algorithms and conduct experiments. Currently, the global IBM Q Network has twelve founding members including the University of Melbourne, JPMorgan Chase, Daimler AG, Samsung, JSR Corporation (a leading chemical and materials company in Japan), Barclays, Hitachi Metals, Honda, Nagase (a leading Japanese chemicals firm),

Japan's Keio University, Oak Ridge National Lab and UK's Oxford University.

Similarly, Microsoft Australia is co-locating its global Station Q quantum at the University of Sydney's Nanoscience Hub to develop a new generation of quantum computing technology. It is hoped that this new technology will contribute to solving some of the current global issues such as climate change, disease cures and cyber-security. Currently, Amazon, following Microsoft's $1 billion investment in the University of Washington to create a pipeline of skilled graduates for the company, is looking to find a university hub for its second headquarters. One of the company's requirements is reported to be a strong pool of talented students who are likely to go into technical fields (Chatlani 2018).

Universities are vital in providing expertise to help communities survive the drastic disruptions that are reshaping our economy. One prominent example is the transformation of rural areas. In their book *The Smartest Places on Earth* (Van Agtmael & Bakker 2016), the authors reported a transformative pattern in more than forty-five previously struggling regional economies in the US and Europe. These places, described as "rust belts", are being turned into "brain belts". In Akron, a midwestern city in Ohio, four tyre companies suddenly closed down. The President of the University of Akron, Dr Luis Proenza, reached out to those affected by the closure and encouraged them to transform their skills. In the end, the retrenched workers helped create a world class hub of polymer companies, outperforming the former tyre companies. The authors remarked that in each of these cases of "rust belt" renewal, the key is the presence of a university which is critical for the transformation success.

In Australia, Siemens is joining force with the Australian Industry Group, a peak employer organisation representing national industry, to reinvent apprenticeships at Melbourne's Swinburne University of Technology. The Chair and CEO of Siemens Australia and New Zealand is also the Chair of Australian Prime Minister's Industry 4.0 Taskforce. The University received a substantial Hi-tech Digitalisation grant of $135m from Siemens for Australia's first Industry 4.0 "Factory of the Future" facility on its campus, to prepare workforce-ready graduates. The innovative initiative will provide higher-level education and required skills to a broad section of young people in Australia. Siemens, along with related companies, will help students achieve qualifications and acquire high-level technology skills through the delivery of a new Diploma and Associate Degree in Applied Technologies at Swinburne University of Technology. The program utilizes the best of university and vocational learning models to impart Science, Technology, Engineering and Maths skills and business design understanding to help students acquire the needed skills for the Fourth Industrial Revolution.

Another model of learning with industry is the concept of a Learning Factory. For Example, the Learning Factory at the Pennsylvania State University is an innovative approach to integrating design and manufacturing into the engineering curriculum. It has a hands-on facility for engineering students to work on industry-related projects. The Learning Factory is a culmination of a deep university-industry partnership where students, faculty and industry sponsor work together to ensure the University produce world-class engineers.

OPEN INNOVATION

To remain competitive in the 21st century, industry has transitioned from closed to open innovation. As the development of innovative products increases in speed and complexity, it requires integration of technologies from many sectors. Knowledge from research partners and networks has become critical for working with increasing complexities and sophistication in product development. The open innovation model involves companies accessing external knowledge for integration with internal know-how. The concept of open innovation was first formulated by Professor Henry Chesbrough at the Haas School of Business at University of California Berkeley in his 2003 book, *Open Innovation: The New Imperative for Creating and Profiting from Technology*. The open innovation paradigm can be understood as the antithesis of the traditional vertically-integrated, closed innovation model (Chesbrough 2012). Open innovation is the "use of purposive inflows and outflows of knowledge to accelerate internal innovation and expand the markets for external use of innovation" (Chesbrough 2006). The future of open innovation will see a more extensive, collaborative engagement between a wider variety of participants, and universities will be pivotal in this trend.

CHAPTER 21

Technology Challenges

Abstract: This chapter looks at the advances in learning technology to stimulate deeper learning in students. These include the use of artificial intelligence (AI), natural language processing, pattern and speech recognition, and robotics. AI can monitor class performance, provide personalized learning support to students, and create an immersive learning experience through the use of virtual or augmented reality. Augmented and virtual reality are useful in helping students understand situations which are difficult to visualise. Virtual reality (VR) can assist students to practice without physical limitations.

Keywords: Artificial Intelligence (AI), Augmented and Virtual Reality, DeakinSync, IBM's Supercomputer Watson, Labster, Teacherbots.

In the last few decades, universities accelerated the adoption of technology into blended learning and collaborative learning, with a view to stimulating deeper learning. They are fast improving their digital literacy in integrating formal and informal learning, improving access and convenience for students. Now the challenge is to rethink the roles of educators and in managing knowledge obsolescence. In the next two to five years, there will be even greater technology adoption in the Internet of Things (IoT) and in the new generation of Learning Management System (LMS), artificial intelligence (AI) and natural user interface. Technology adoption is fostering authentic learning through the use of pedagogies such as project-based learning, creating a more hands-on, real-world experience for students. Instead of being passive learners, students are becoming active contributors to the knowledge system. In addition to making textbooks and learning resources electronically available and interactive with quizzes, technology can enhance learning in many dimensions. The primary purpose of these learning technologies is to improve learning outcome and enhance the student's learning experience. More and more universities are using AI for these purposes. AI includes a range of scientific applications such as machine learning, natural language processing, pattern and speech recognition, and robotics. AI can monitor class performance, provide personalized learning support to students, and create an immersive learning experience through the use of virtual or augmented reality. Augmented reality is particularly useful in helping students understand situations which are difficult to visualise, such as environments in the body at a cellular level. The use technology can help students and researchers to experiment in different scenarios and test out hypotheses. Virtual reality (VR) can assist students to practice without physical limitations or incurring safety issues in fields such as surgical operations and pilot training. VR is already being used in fields as diverse as medicine, architecture and law to create a virtual world of cells, buildings or case scenarios.

ARTIFICIAL INTELLIGENCE (AI)

For decades, there have been tremendous efforts to make machines more human-like, in the quest to make them work more intelligently for us. We want machines to be more intuitive, and behave and think more like us. Research into the human brain and neural networks has helped researchers to replicate some of our learning and adaption abilities within machines. Capabilities such as deep machine learning and pattern recognition are enhancing advances in AI research. With the explosion of computer power, areas such as machine and deep learning, sensor detection, computer vision, robotics and automation have been advancing rapidly. AI applications are used in natural language processing such as translation, video analytics, biometrics, and facial and behavioral recognition. In pursuing AI, the goal is to simulate human intelligence and learning in a machine, minimizing the need for human input. AI computing systems can engage in human-like processes such as learning, adapting, synthesizing, self-correction, and using data for complex processing tasks. In a 2017 article published by the Wharton School of the University of Pennsylvania, Andrew Ng, the co-founder of Coursera and an adjunct Stanford professor who founded the Google Brain Deep Learning Project, described AI as "the new electricity," transforming every major industry just as electricity did a century ago (Knowledge@Wharton 2017). But even with all the advances in deep machine learning, AI is still no match for the human brain. Human intelligence has a tremendous ability to experiment, learn and test solutions in parallel and incrementally, from the quantum level to planetary scale, in a self-modified manner (Bently 2017).

Advances in AI create new possibilities and challenges for teaching and learning in universities, with the potential to fundamentally change the academic architecture and governance. For example, IBM's supercomputer Watson provides student advice 24/7 for Deakin University in Australia. Watson has digested massive amount of information from the University's unstructured data to provide students with consistent, high-quality answers in natural language through the university's DeakinSync online hub. Watson also partners with another institution, the University of Southampton, in its Curriculum Innovation programme. IBM has now set up its own IBM Global University Programs, with an IBM Skills Academy offering courses in cognitive technology, data science and analytics, and quantum computing.

Virtual Reality is taking immersive learning to new heights. Based on the idea behind flight simulators, Michael Bodekaer created a virtual laboratory called Labster, to revolutionize science teaching, making it twice as effective and engaging with students. He found from his own experience that students were bored with traditional methods of science teaching and many did not even understand why they were studying a specific topic. Many of the existing education technologies on the market, such as online content and learning management systems, merely provide an alternative medium of delivery without actually engaging students in a meaningful and practical ways. Bonde *et al.* (2014) demonstrated that gamified laboratory simulations using Labster motivated students and improved learning outcomes compared with traditional teaching approaches. The researchers discovered a high level of motivation (97%) and engagement with the Labster simulation. This study indicates that a gamified laboratory simulation can significantly enhance science learning when compared with, and especially when combined with, traditional teaching.

Another example of VR revolutionizing education is the Virtual Reality Anatomy Lab at Colorado State University. Using cutting-edge VR and augmented reality technology, students are able to manipulate magnified models of the human brain and the nervous system. They can visualize the functional signaling of neural networks in all dimensions (Maze 2017).

The Institute for Simulation & Training at the University of Central Florida partners with Boeing to train pilots through the use of virtual pilot and co-pilot. The program creates a pilot avatar, modeled on a real-life pilot but can be customized, in different genders, cultures and languages. With the help of virtual-reality goggles, students can have an immersive virtual flying experience and have the opportunity to interact with the virtual co-pilot just as in real-life flying.

One of the key challenges facing university leaders is the need for redesign of physical campus space due to the impact of fast-moving technology. Physical environments must be continuously reconfigured and restructured. With each pedagogical shift, mew infrastructure has to be put in place for collaboration, visualization and digital connection (Horizon Report 2017). University leaders should also be mindful that strategic investment in technologies such as VR will increasingly become a differentiator in student choice. The challenge for university leaders is to implement a VR strategy and implementation plan which builds or adds to institutional capabilities.

This technology-enabled reality will require university leaders to reimagine their business models. As AI can provide, guide, monitor student learning, the role of the educator will need to be reframed (Popenici & Kerr 2017). Teacherbots are becoming a disruptive alternative to traditional teachers. However, nothing can replace a passionate, gifted human teacher who enchants, inspires and creates lasting memories for students.

AI cannot completely replace the kind of general intelligence that humans have. Computers have yet to demonstrate that they can apply intuition-based decision-making in relation to specific situations in the classroom. AI can substitute for a number of administrative functions and provide basic teaching assistance, but it does not in itself encourage freedom of thinking and in-depth understanding. In the spirit of promoting creativity, initiative, and entrepreneurialism for graduates, the job of inspiring students rests with talented teachers.

CHAPTER 22

Reinventing the University Business Model

Abstract: To pursue its academic goals, a university adopts a business model to fund its operation. This involves defining the university's value proposition to society, its offerings to students, cost structures, and the revenue streams needed to run the institution. But universities are facing many challenges to their current value proposition. Students and employers are questioning the value of an expensive higher education. Universities themselves are also having financing and resourcing problems. Furthermore, the productivity and efficiency of universities are increasingly under scrutiny. Changing demand from local and international students, along with technology transformation and unprecedented competition from newcomers, makes a compelling case for universities to reimagine their business models. The impact of online learning, especially from the private sector, challenges the traditional business model of bricks-and-mortar public universities. The lower costs, flexibility and fast response time presented by MOOCs seriously threatens the traditional market of universities.

Keywords: Business Model, Coursera, edX, Digital Badges, Disruption, High-Margin Courses, Learning Store, Low-Margin Courses, Micro-Credentials, MicroMasters, MOOCs, Nanodegree, OpenCourseWare, Pricing Model, Value Proposition.

The two main missions of universities are to educate and to advance knowledge. Translating these missions into business operations requires viable operating models to ensure long-term sustainability. In management-speak, a business model refers to the way a university funds its operation in order to pursue academic goals. This involves defining the university's value proposition to society, its offerings to students, cost structures, and the revenue streams needed to run the institution. Underlying economic logic explains how a university can deliver value to society at an appropriate cost. It includes identifying the university's distinctive resources and capabilities, strengths and weaknesses, competitors and collaborators, student segments, technology and delivery.

Universities are facing many challenges to their current value proposition. Students and employers are questioning the value of an expensive higher education. Universities themselves are also having financing and resourcing problems: declining public funding; tuition fee reaching a peak; eroding public trust; and close scrutiny of education quality. Furthermore, the productivity and efficiency of universities, and cross-subsidisation between teaching and research, are increasingly under the microscope. Changing demand from local and international students, along with technology transformation and unprecedented competition from newcomers, makes a compelling case for universities to reimagine their business models. The impact of online learning, especially from the private sector, challenges the traditional business model of bricks-and-mortar public universities. The lower costs, flexibility and fast response time presented by MOOCs seriously threatens the traditional market of universities. In particular, the expanding numbers of alternative credentials offered by specialized businesses erodes the market share of conventional universities. Unfortunately, not many universities have the rich financial resources and reputation to withstand this wave unscathed. Disruptive market forces may result in a major overhaul of the higher education landscape, leaving few survivors.

Across the Western world, public funding for universities is declining. At the same time, domestic student enrolments are stagnating or falling in accordance with aging populations. Increasing tuition fees is not a long-term option, since many students already find higher education unaffordable. Many universities are recruiting international students to make up the shortfall. Whatever the source of students, universities will need to look at how to run their organizations sustainably, by doing more with less.

The US Presidential Innovation Lab, *Beyond the Inflection Point: Reimagining Business Models for Higher Education* (Presidential Innovation Papers), has warned that universities can no longer rely on increasing financial support from governments, due to the decline in state appropriations for public higher education. It recommended a three-pronged approach: maintaining fee revenue streams; containing costs; and rethinking pricing models. However, with enrolments and fee levels remaining flat for the foreseeable future, universities cannot rely on the continuing growth of tuition revenue. Therefore, universities need to do all they can to at least maintain this revenue stream by actively recruiting quality students and retaining them with a good value proposition, *i.e.*, high-quality teaching and learning outcomes. They also need to be diligent about cutting their administrative expenditure and containing costs.

In addition, an overhaul of pricing models is urgently needed, since most universities simply set fees according to students' willingness to pay relative to their university competitors. Now competition is coming from outside the university system: private providers, industry, and professional bodies can undercut university tuition fees since they are not burdened by huge administrative costs.

Another challenge relates to the fact that universities often use high-margin courses to subsidise low-margin courses which are more expensive to run. This practice will not be sustainable if enrolments for high-margin courses continue to decline, with students questioning where their fees have gone. The same threat also applies to the cross-subsidization between teaching and research, meaning research activities will not be sustainable if they are not conducted efficiently or funded adequately. In the past, university strategies have been based on the assumption of an institution growing bigger and better. This may no longer be an achievable goal and many universities are deliberately growing smaller and more specialized in order to differentiate themselves.

To redesign their business models, universities should review their mix of offerings and services, revenue generation mechanisms, cost structures and utilization of assets. In essence, it must look for ways to reduce costs and find sustainable revenue streams. With declining prospects in revenue growth, cost containment and efficiency enhancement will be critical. University leaders need to think creatively about delivering the best value and services to students at the lowest cost. The focus is not just on cost-cutting but on operational efficiency. University leaders should review all of their cost drivers to ensure that expenditures align directly with its academic mission. This will require a complete redesign of institutional processes and assumptions in relation to framing budgets. All options should be on the table: outsourcing, shared services and partnership, asset optimization and recycling, leasing instead of purchasing; tracking expenses against jobs, reviewing suppliers' cost options, leveraging technology such as automation and AI. Asset-recycling can be used to enable universities to lease under-utilized infrastructure assets and reinvest the proceeds in new and necessary infrastructure projects.

Bearing in mind in this climate of graduate underemployment, skills mismatch, industry automation, and increasing public expectation, universities must create compelling value for students of the 21ˢᵗ century. They can no longer rely on their past reputations or the promise of credentials. Other disruptive providers can do as much, but at a lower cost. Universities cannot blame governance and regulations for their rigid academic structures and timetable-driven classes. They need to shift from a supplier mindset to a student-centric vision. That is, they will need to co-create their delivery models with their students.

Students do not necessarily want to be confined to rigid schedules. They expect learning materials to be delivered to their mobile devices anywhere, anytime. Yet, as discussed in the previous section, students value engagement with their teachers. They want to go beyond a transactional relationship with their universities. They want to play an active part in their learning journeys and expect their universities to put their interests first. The challenge for a university is to provide a supportive learning environment with caring staff. It is essential to create a sense of belonging and connectedness with students.

In reimagining university business models, there are lessons to be learned from entrepreneurial leaders such as Apple's Steve Jobs. For Apple to achieve its spectacular success, Isaacson (2012) has identified a number of keys to Jobs' approach: stay focused; simplify things and eliminate the unnecessary; make things seamlessly integrated; innovate and advance; be wary of appearance; work only with the best; and pursuit for perfection. Many of these principles are extremely relevant to universities.

For example to stay focused is to concentrate on the institution's unique strengths: say, its top 30 programs or top five research areas with an international reputation. In the past, universities have allowed their programs to proliferate. They offer a vast range of programs, driven by supply, many of which do not result in real jobs. Furthermore, having a huge number of programs adds to administrative costs. In selecting the top programs, appropriate criteria need to be used, such as student outcomes including employability and career paths, market demands, and anticipated future skills needs. Top research fields should be benchmarked globally, with excellent researchers fully supported to allow them to focus on innovation and discovery.

As the domestic workforce becomes more educated, there will be greater demand for professional development. Universities should take advantage of the need for lifelong learning and offer postgraduate taught programs targeted at workforce needs. Delivering programs of shorter duration at lower costs or online micro-credentials would be attractive to mature-age students. There are tremendous opportunities for universities to partner with industries to provide workforce solutions and address skill shortages.

Micro-credentials, also known as *digital badges*, are generally offered in short, intensive and flexible modes outside the normal academic program. They are highly portable and cater primarily to professional development. They tend to be highly specialized and focus on emerging cutting-edge technologies which have not become mainstream in universities' academic offerings. They are very flexible: available online, on-campus, or as a mixture of modes. Since they are usually credit-bearing, learners have the options to stack their micro-credentials towards a diploma or degree program. As such, micro-credentials provide a pathway into for-credit degrees and improve access to equal opportunity for all students to succeed. As many micro-credentials have an industry focus and are recognised by industry, they serve to fill skill gaps in the workforce. There has been a growth of micro-credentials in data science, AI, big data, and blockchain to address the skills shortage in the emerging technologies market.

While many Micro-credentials are offered through MOOCs, some are actually offered by businesses. For example, IBM offers courses in cognitive technology, data science and analytics, the Internet of Things, and quantum computing. The MOOC provider EdX now offers over 30 MicroMasters programs from top universities such as MIT, Columbia and University of Pennsylvania. These MicroMasters provide deep, accelerated learning in very specialized areas and focus on industry-relevant skills. They are recognized by industry leaders including General Electric, Volvo, Bloomberg, PWC, and Ford. Learners can use these MicroMasters as credits towards an accelerated and less costly Master's degree in universities which recognise MicroMasters programs.

The educational organization Udacity offers Nanodegree Plus, which has a money-back guarantee for employment within six months of graduation. It offers Nanodegrees in machine learning, virtual reality, robotics, web development, data analysis, and autonomous flight systems. All study materials are co-created with industry partners such as Google, Facebook, Amazon, IBM, nvidia, Samsung, Tableau and DiDi. Udacity has also collaborated with Georgia Technology University and AT&T, the world's largest telecommunications company, to offer an online Master's program in Computer Science. AT&T also offers scholarships *via* Udacity for nanodegrees in computer programming, web development and Android basics.

Coursera, one of America's leading MOOC developers, offers over 2000 courses with more than 140 top international universities. It delivers wide-ranging courses from STEM to humanities and business courses. In 2017, Coursera had 24 million registered users signed up to its programs. It has formed partnerships with Google, Instagram and other companies for its microdegrees.

It is clear that online programs are becoming serious competitors for higher education. The collaboration between MOOCs and employers will be a game-changer, posing further threats to the university model. In the spirit of unbundling services, some universities are starting to use the micro-credentials model, disaggregating their multi-year rigid academic architecture into short, low-cost online courses.

The University of Wisconsin-Extension, Georgia Institute of Technology, University of Washington-Extension, University of California Irvine Extension, University of California Davis Extension, and University of California Los

Angeles Extension have formed a consortium called The Learning Store, where they offer a number of business-focused short courses. These universities recognised that the rapid pace of changes requires workers to pursue lifelong learning and upskill in order to remain employable and competitive in a global job market. They have designed these low-cost affordable courses that workers can complete in days or weeks rather than years. These credentials are competency-based and verified by employers.

The current Governor of California, Jerry Brown, wants to impose tuition freezes on his state's two university systems, but he is also willing to invest in a fully online community college (Kelderman 2018). The aim is to provide flexible learning and professional development for 2.5 million adults. It is hoped that the online courses will have a competency-based approach to help students to acquire work-relevant skills. There are similar systems at the University of Wisconsin system and SUNY (State University of New York).

The Massachusetts Institute of Technology OpenCourseWare initiative (MITx) provides free open access to class lecture notes, exams and videos. It has the ambitious goal of reaching a billion people by 2021. MITx also delivers online courses and MicroMasters through the MOOC provider EdX. Upon completion of a MicroMasters credential, students can apply for accelerated entry to a masters degree program at MIT. MITx courses embody the signature features of MIT and are based on its residential courses. MIT has a noble vision to provide knowledge to humanity as the University recognises that human potential is universal but opportunity is not.

CHAPTER 23

Taming the Management Boogeyman

Abstract: Corporate management is ill-suited for managing knowledge workers such as academics. Current generation of university managers are relying on antiquated command and control management methods. However, while work that are relatively structured may be relegated to AI, attention should be focused on non-standard creative work that does not lend itself to being managed.

Keywords: Command and Control Management, Key Performance Measurements, Knowledge Workers, Positional Power.

The concept of corporate management is obsolete in the VUCA era (Chakhoyan 2017). It is an archaic practice, left over from the Second Industrial Revolution. But many universities are still ruled by outmoded organisational and management structures. The tyranny of positional power, policies and procedures is stifling the spirit of innovation in universities. Why do universities recruit talented people only to strangle them with rigid organisational structures and starve them of resources? Today, work that requires supervision should be outsourced to AI, while non-standard creative work does not lend itself to being managed. Even so, many university managers amass power by proliferating divisions of labour, thereby multiplying the bureaucratic divisions under their authority.

Corporate management is ill-suited for managing knowledge workers such as academics. This is particularly so when many of the current generation of university managers and leaders are still reliant on antiquated command and control management methods, similar to those used in the last century for factory workers. These managers force metrics, Key Performance measurements, and so-called values and behaviour expectations on their knowledge workers. In addition, many university managers rely on consultants to do their jobs instead of seeking help from experts within their own organization. For instance, at one university, a one-page simplification principles document generated by staff with the intention of getting rid of some of the bureaucracy was turned into a 400-page document which cost the university over $ 6 million in consultancy fees – and nobody uses it. This is a very common trend in universities. If they encounter a problem, managers immediately call for consultants since they are distrustful of their own staff, particularly the academics. Another common approach to problem-solving is to hire a number of mangers responsible for individual tasks without consideration for the cost of overall coordination. These are just a few examples illustrating the incompetence of management in many universities. Instead of making real improvements, they follow whatever trends that is in vogue.

This is the dominant pattern: one initiative starts, but it hardly has a chance to complete before the next fad is rolled out. Instead of nurturing the staff they already have, management insist on poaching high-flyers who simply bide time before the next highest offer comes along. This is why the principles of self-awareness and self-discovery are so essential for a university. Rather than slavishly following trends, universities need to identify their own unique attributes, and accentuate those attributes to differentiate themselves. The imitation of management fads stifles innovation and progress.

With the rapid advancement of AI technologies, especially through the judicious deployment of deep learning and text mining techniques, work that is relatively structured may be handled by AI knowledge-based algorithms. In this way, meetings and committees may be streamlined, while manual management decision-making and interventions are minimized, so that the process becomes more transparent and predictable.

CHAPTER 24

Budget Challenge

Abstract: National governments are reducing their financial support to universities and are determined to tame the tuition tiger. They want financial transparency and universities to control their administrative costs as a priority. Zero-Based Mindset is a novel way of looking at cost efficiency through four zero-based approaches. Universities have to go beyond financial sustainability and include social and environmental performance to account for the full cost in doing business.

Keywords: Triple bottom line, Zero-based Front Office, Zero-based Mindset, Zero-based Organization, Zero-based Spend, Zero-based Supply Chain.

The US Education Department's National Center for Education Statistics data has shown that many universities are under increasing financial pressures. The number of colleges and universities eligible to award federal financial aid to their students dropped by 5.6 percent from 2015-16 to 2016-17: the sixth straight year of decline (Lederman 2017, Fain 2017). The Governor of California wants to impose tuition freezes for the state's two university systems. Also, following the political criticism over the University of California system's size, cost and budget practices, the University President is planning to streamline her office with a drastic 50% ($438 million) budget cut (Watanabe 2018).

The Australian Government is also cutting $2.2bn from its universities, mainly through a two-year freeze in Commonwealth teaching grants. Although it does not directly reverse the demand-driven policy of capping student places, the Australian Government's freeze on funding will nevertheless put pressure on universities to limit their government-funded enrolments. The Education Minister, Simon Birmingham, says universities should not be complaining about funding reform while they have allowed their overheads grow faster than revenue. He blames the universities for choosing to maintain their huge administration and marketing budgets rather than find the needed efficiencies (Bolton 2018). The Australian Government's expenditure on higher education escalated when the previous Labor Government removed limits on university enrolments in 2012. As a consequence, universities expanded their enrolments unrestrainedly, resulting in the Government having to provide $8.5 billion to higher education each year, with an additional $8 billion as income-contingent loans to students. However, student repayments only reached $1.9 billion in 2014, and it was projected that doubtful debts would remain at around 19%. In fact, recent figures show that Australian university student debt has surged to a record AUD 47.8 billion, up 20% from the year before and more than double the AUD 22.6 billion owed in 2010-2011 (Dodd & Mather 2017). There are nearly 11,000 graduates, who each owe the government more than AUD 100,000. Even so, some universities openly admitted that they would not be absorbing the funding cuts and that it was acceptable for students to contribute more to their education because of the private gain they expect in getting better, higher-paid jobs (Hare 2017).

In the UK, the Government has frozen university tuition fees at the current level of £9,250 for the 2018/19 academic year with immediate effect, while raising the income threshold for loan repayment from £21,000 to £25,000 a year (Adams & Mason 2017).

The US has also made efforts to tame the tuition tiger. The US House Committee on Education and the Workforce has told the Council for Higher Education Accreditation that there will be no additional resources for higher education, and that institutions have to become more efficient (Foxx & Feulner 2018). The Committee felt that the US economy has been hampered by two problems concerning higher education. One is the massive student loan debt, which has ballooned to $1.4 trillion. The second is that some of these debts have been incurred by students who dropped out before completing a degree, but even many of those who managed to graduate still found themselves underemployed. Despite generous government subsidies over the past decades, it believes that colleges continue to squander and take advantage of increases in student aid. The Government also plans to eliminate loan forgiveness programs. At the time of writing, graduates can have their loans forgiven 20 years after college if they enter government work, or 10 years if they take non-profit jobs.

Mr C Thomas McMillen, former regent of University of Maryland System and former U.S. Representative, 4th District of Maryland, advises that university governing boards need timely financial data to enable them to accurately benchmark their universities against others, and determine how the institutions can be leaner while keeping tuition low and quality high. The American Council of Trustees and Alumni (ACTA) 2017 guide on "How Much is Too Much? Controlling Administrative Costs through Effective Oversight" encourages discussion between governing board members and the senior leadership about their university's financial priorities. How does our university's spending on administration compared with that of other institutions? Does our university spend enough on the number-one priorities of teaching and learning? Can our university, given its existing resources, do more for our students? (ACTA 2017). Universities have a moral obligation to make sure that fees paid by students and their parents, as well as taxpayer funds, are properly deployed. The purpose of the Guide is to help governing boards hold their universities accountable to the public trust.

The control of administrative costs should be a priority as it heavily affects the cost of tuition and, in turn, access. A 2017 report by the US Institute for Higher Education Policy shows that tuition fees at 70% of US universities are unaffordable for working- and middle-class students, even with the maximum level of federal financial aid. It found that "the crisis in college costs and affordability is undermining the democratic promise of higher education" (ACTA 2017 p 2). A 2014 College Governance Survey commissioned by the American Council of Trustees and Alumni also found that an overwhelming 91% of respondents believed that the governing boards needed to act to make college more affordable and improve its quality. The study also found a severe imbalance of resources: the percentage of faculty has declined drastically in relation to the rise of administration. Administrative growth is found to have an inverse relationship to institutional efficiency, and it raises issues of institutional priorities, public perception, and staff morale. The public is justified in looking to university governing boards to address this problem. They want the governing boards to monitor how well the mission of teaching and learning is resourced.

NOWHERE TO HIDE: THE NEED FOR FINANCIAL TRANSPARENCY

Education is Australia's third largest export, but this success has come at a cost. Funding has increased by 71% since 2009, at twice the rate of economic growth (Australian Government 2017). An analysis by the accounting firm Deloitte has found that while the average funding for universities per student increased by 15% between 2010 and 2015, the cost for universities to deliver courses has only gone up by 9.5%. This finding is based on a detailed study by Deloitte Access Economics commissioned by the Australian Government. The study collected detailed data from 17 universities on the cost of teaching in 19 fields of education. The study found that the majority of the education areas recorded funding exceeding costs in all but a few areas such as dentistry and veterinary studies.

The Deloitte report also found universities generating an average profit margin of over 5%, with some universities recording significant surpluses of over $100 million. It was observed that universities were influenced to some degree in expanding areas of education where funding matched or exceeded the cost of provision. The Australian Government also pointed out that the vice-chancellors' salaries have soared over recent years, with nine vice-chancellors receiving annual salaries of over $1 million in 2015, and this number has increased to eleven in

2017 (Knott 2017). Some Australia vice-chancellors were paid more than the Vice-Chancellor of the University of Oxford, more than twice the salary of the Australian Prime Minister, and ten times more than the average academic lecturer (Houghton 2016). The average remuneration package of Australian university vice-chancellors was close to $900,000 in 2015.

In a comparative analysis conducted by Times Higher Education in 2014-2015, the Vice-Chancellor of the University of Oxford was paid less than the vice-chancellors of twenty-one Australian universities. While Australian universities are crying poor over government funding cuts, their executive remuneration certainly seem overgenerous. Consequently, the Australian Government will impose a two-year freeze on the maximum amount of funding provided through the Commonwealth Grant Scheme. Any Commonwealth Grant Scheme funding increases from 2020 onwards will be linked to performance and national growth in the 18-64 year old population (Birmingham 2017).

In the UK, vice-chancellors' salaries are also under scrutiny. A report released by the University and College Union disclosed that 23 UK universities had increased their vice-chancellors' salaries by 10% or more in 2015-16. 55 vice-chancellors had salaries of over £300,000 a year, and eleven had salaries of over £400,000 (Khomami 2017). There is a call for restraint on university executive payments, whose largesse stands in stark contrast to the stagnant pay and worsening conditions for academic staff and the unprecedented levels of current student debt.

ZERO-BASED MINDSET

The Zero-Based mindset (ZBx), designed by the global professional service Accenture (Timmermans & Abdalla 2017), is a novel way of looking at cost efficiency through four zero-based approaches. Zero-Based budgeting (ZBB) is a management method of containing costs. In order to cut unnecessary costs, it requires an organization to set its budget to zero each year rather than base them on historical expenditures. It imposes stricter controls and rigorous governance. The Zero-Based approach has been widely and successful adopted at many global companies. After overcoming initial implementation challenges, many companies have found the multi-dimensional strategy rewarding, resulting in improved competitiveness, profitability, growth, and trust. The surplus generated allows organizations to invest in strategic initiatives.

ZBx is about improving organisational agility. It has four areas of intervention: Zero-based spend, Zero-based organization, Zero-based front office, and Zero-based supply chain. Zero-based spend (ZBS) enables organizations to closely examine the discretionary spend of overhead expenses so that university leadership can make the right choices to change the spending culture and ultimately freeing up funds. Zero-based organization (ZBO) allows the university leadership to redesign the organization from a clean base, moving talents from non-productive work to strategic areas in response to environmental opportunities. Zero-based front office (ZBFO) optimizes student-facing administrative services to deliver superior student outcomes. Lastly, Zero-based supply chain (ZBSC) identifies the direct costs of teaching and research, ensuring that expenditure has a direct, positive impact on academic goals.

THINKING BEYOND: THE TRIPLE BOTTOM LINE

The term "triple bottom line" was coined by John Elkington in 1994. It proposes that in order to ensure the sustainability of an organization, it is necessary to go beyond financial sustainability. Organizations also need to be measured against their social and environmental responsibilities. Thus, the triple bottom line consists of three Ps: profit, people and planet, in taking the financial, social and environmental performance of the organization to account for the full cost in doing business. In their latest book, Szekely & Dossa (2017) expands the triple bottom line model to include mission and purpose, long-term vision, stakeholder engagement, transparency and governance, and sustainability innovation. These are all within the remit of universities.

CHAPTER 25

Changing Student Demographics

Abstract: While domestic student numbers are declining in developed countries, international student enrolments have grown and will continue to grow. But the source and destination countries will change based on capacity, political and economic factors. However, universities should not simply rely on inflow of affluent international students as home country governments are waking up to the outflow of financial and human capitals. Instead, universities should genuinely invest in enhancing internationalization of education and explore new models of partnerships for mutual benefits.

Keywords: Demographics, International Students, Multilateral Partnerships, Student Mobility.

While most developed countries will see a decline or stagnation of domestic university student enrolments due to lower birth rates, there will be significant growths in higher education in the emerging countries. StudyPortals, an online global education choice platform and research organization, has recently released a report on the megatrends in higher education and international student mobility (Choudaha & Van Rest 2018). Based on analysis of the statistics of 15 high-income countries, the report projected an overall growth of 56% in higher education enrolment over the period of 2015 to 2030. During the same period, international higher education enrolment is predicted to grow by 51%. A 1% growth in international student enrolments result in 412,000 extra international student enrolments in the 15 high-income countries. Furthermore, a 1% annual increase of non-traditional students (over the age of 24) in the high-income countries would translate into 4.3 million additional enrolments. As a whole, the report predicted that by 2030, there will be 323 million higher education students, an increase of nearly 120 million from 2015. Based on the OECD's 2017 Education at a Glance, 5.6% of total university enrolments were international students, a third of them studying STEM subjects, and just over a quarter studying business, administration or law. Students from Asia (53%) form the largest group of international tertiary students undertaking study abroad.

On the other hand, the increasing capacity and ambition of universities in Asia and emerging countries will shift the market dynamics of global higher education. The latest research from the British Council's *International student mobility to 2027: Local investment, global outcomes* predicts a slowing of outbound student growth in these countries in the next decade, estimating it at 1.7% per year comparing to the average annual growth of 6% between 2000 and 2015. While China and India have been unmatched in terms of their scale and growth as source countries in the past decade, their domestic investments in higher education will see a slowing of outbound mobility. University leaders need to look at diversifying their international student sources and investing in emerging markets such as Indonesia, Nigeria, Pakistan, Nepal, Bangladesh, Kenya and Europe.

The number of international students travelling to a destination country is affected by a number of factors such as tuition fees and the cost of living, employment and immigration prospects, and the political relationship between the sending and receiving countries. A 2017 IDP Education survey on International Student Buyer Behaviour Research has found that Australia is getting overly expensive in its tuition fees and cost of living. While the US and UK are considered to have the best education, they are also becoming unaffordable. There are safety concerns regarding studying in the US and UK, and their onerous visa requirements pose a barrier. On the other hand, Canada and New Zealand seem to offer a more affordable education, easier visa requirements, and a safe environment.

The current US political climate and its travel ban are sending an unwelcoming message to international students. The Council of Graduate Schools reported an overall 3% decline in applications and 1% drop in commencements in 2017. A sharper drop was observed in Masters and Doctoral programs (Redden 2017). Despite political tensions, China remains the number one source market, accounting for a third of foreign student enrolment in US graduate schools, while India maintains its second position at 25% of total enrolment. Despite the declining trends, US is still the leading international study destination, with over a million international students in 2017. This has huge benefits for the country – according to the US Department of Commerce, international students brought $39.4 billion to the US economy in 2016.

Unfortunately, international students are no panacea for declining enrolment in the US, since the number of students accepting admission offers has also declined. The decline has been sharpest from markets in India, followed by Brazil and Saudi Arabia, possibly due to the new US government policies. Even the growth of Chinese international student numbers has slowed from double digits to around 7%. The weakened US international student market has benefited Canada and Australia. The number of international students in Canadian universities grew by 20% in 2016. Australia has also seen continuing growth in its international student market (Fischer 2017).

Nevertheless, universities should not simply rely on the inflow of affluent international students to fill the revenue gap, as home country governments are waking up to the outflow of financial and human capitals. Instead, universities should genuinely invest in enhancing internationalization of education; and explore new models of partnerships for mutual benefits. Indeed, multilateral partnerships involving universities are springing up in China and Asia. For example, the Tsinghua - UC Berkeley Shenzhen Institute was established through the three-party collaboration between Tsinghua University, UC-Berkeley and the Shenzhen government. The Institute's aim is to promote global research collaboration and graduate student education in Environment Science and New Energy Technology, Information Technology and Data science, and Precision Medicine and Healthcare. The institute seeks to integrate research programs at both UC Berkeley and Tsinghua University to address societal needs and global challenges.

CHAPTER 26

Crisis Management

Abstract: Crises can occur without notice, from anywhere at any time. They can pose serious threats to a university's safety, reputation and community standing. Crisis leadership is becoming an important function of the university president. But crisis leadership cannot be delegated to subordinates, since critical decisions should rest with the university president who is ultimately accountable for managing the crisis. Crises are complex and dynamic, involving multiple stakeholders, and could have unanticipated flow-on implications for the university's reputation. Crisis leadership comprises six distinct but interrelated functions: preparation which facilitates collaboration and coordination, effectively interpreting the complex context of the incident, decision-making for a rapid and targeted response, communication to stakeholders and constituents, and learning from the crisis.

Keywords: Crisis Management, Cybersecurity Risk Management, Emergency Preparedness, Freedom of Expression, Homeland Security, Incident Command System (ICS), National Incident Management System (NIMS).

While most universities have some type of emergency management and business continuity plan, many university leaders have not received adequate training in handling crises. Crises can occur without notice, from anywhere at any time. They may take the form of natural disasters, catastrophic weather conditions, fires, epidemics and pandemics, power blackouts, infrastructure breakdown, accidents, deliberate attacks and terrorism, cybersecurity breaches, campus riots and protests, as well as serious threats to a university's reputation and community standing. Crisis leadership is becoming an important function of the university president – several presidents have recently been forced to resign due to their mishandling of campus crises.

A crisis is defined as an incident when the university leader experiences a serious threat to the functioning and reputation of the university under highly uncertain circumstances and time-critical pressure, when crucial decisions need to be made. In the US, there is the National Incident Management System (NIMS) and the Incident Command System (ICS) to assist university leaders to be prepared for such emergencies. There are also crisis management tools in the areas of effective risk management, decision-making, and communication.

It is important to note that crisis leadership cannot be delegated to subordinates, since critical decisions should rest with the university president who is ultimately accountable for managing the crisis. Crises are different from operational emergencies. They are more complex and dynamic, involving multiple stakeholders, and could have unanticipated flow-on implications for the university's reputation.

University campuses should be open and accessible, but open dialogue and passionate debate can flare up into confrontations. University campuses in the US have seen an increasing number of incidents leading to widespread campus dissatisfaction, some resulting in the ultimate departure of the presidents. As a consequence, there are now multi-disciplinary teams which look at ways to better manage critical incidents. Their research has found that crisis leadership comprises six distinct but interrelated functions: preparation which facilitates collaboration and coordination, effectively interpreting the complex context of the incident, decision-making for a rapid and targeted response, communication to stakeholders and constituents, and learning from the crisis (Brennan & Stern 2017).

These functions boil down to six main tasks: *preparing, sense-making, decision-making, meaning-making, terminating,* and *learning,* as outlined by Brennan & Stern (2017). Dr. Brennan is Vice-President for Communications and Marketing and Clinical Professor of Business at the State University of New York at Albany, while Professor Stern is at SUNY's College of Emergency Preparedness, Homeland Security and Cybersecurity.

Preparing for crisis leadership concerned the co-ordination of various functions to facilitate a collaborative effort in a crisis. It involves planning, organising, training and practice to ensure key personnel work as a team for effective response. It also includes setting up protocols to determine when to take critical precautionary measures and apply effective intervention where necessary.

Sense-making in crisis leadership refers to the interpretation of what are often complex, dynamic, volatile, uncertain and ambiguous situations. University presidents require great skill in interpreting the evolving narratives, while at the same time leading actual responses to the critical incidents.

Decision-making refers to making crucial decisions in a timely manner under extremely difficult conditions. Frequently, university presidents have to make decisions in crisis situations that are uncertain and still evolving, and which may sometimes conflict with the university's key values.

Meaning-making is the way in which the university president communicates to the various stakeholders and constituencies the meaning of what has happened and places it in a broader perspective. The president can use appropriate language to convey calm, control, and decisiveness as well empathy. They are expected to acknowledge the emotional state of the campus community and provide recommendations for remedial action. It may also be necessary to convene some rituals of solidarity and unity, mourning or commemoration, depending on the circumstances.

Terminating has two components: *ending* and *accounting*. *Ending* is finding the appropriate time to call an end to the crisis state and return the university to normal operations. The timing is important, since attempting to end a crisis hastily could alienate constituencies who may still be in some sort of danger. There may also be continuing recriminations and unresolved conflicts. The work of *accounting* includes submitting the institutional response to the scrutiny of an external body for review and recommendations.

Learning from a crisis is an extremely valuable exercise. It involves producing an analysis of the response to crisis, with a view to improving processes, procedures and mindset in responding to future events. The learning stage must also encompass the examination of the contributing causes of the incident, how circumstances could have been better managed, and how the university could be better prepared for such incidents. True university leaders would ensure that the lessons learned from a crisis would strengthen the university's response capabilities, finding some benefit in adversity.

Recent violent events in a number of American universities have called into question the role of university presidents in addressing instances of extremist activity and unrest on campus. Protests and unrests will continue to occur as student bodies become more politically active and racially diverse. University presidents must start to consider their positions and plan in advance how they are going to handle student activism. They also have an obligation to ensure that other students on campus do not feel unsafe or threatened by violence. It is worth noting that some protests may be initiated by antagonists outside the university, who use the campus as a means to stir up student sentiment.

As protests on campus become a fact of life, some universities have started to see a drop in enrolment. University presidents need to take a stand on freedom of expression without compromising student safety. For example, the Stone Report of the University of Chicago on Freedom of Expression, which is widely adopted by many US universities, states that the university encourages constructive criticism provided such expression does not violate the law, falsely defame or constitute a genuine threat or harassment, or impede the functioning of the university (Stone, Zimmer, Issacs & Levi 2015). While protecting freedom of expression and other human rights, universities have the obligation to demonstrate moral leadership and promote values of global citizenship, community, diversity, tolerance, equality, mutual respect, and peaceful co-existence.

CHAPTER 27

High-Level Leadership

Abstract: This chapter looks at the leadership qualities required to guide complex organizations such as universities. But the unpredictable landscape demands a fresh approach as university presidents are increasingly subject to high resolution and three dimensional scrutiny. Instead of relying on last century's old management mindset, university leaders have to build institutions that are agile and flexible which can learn continuously. They must engage effectively with staff to explain why this culture of flexibility and innovation is critical for institutional survival. The rapidly changing and turbulent environment brought on by politics, society, economy and the environment requires a unique style of leadership - one that focuses on authenticity, systems thinking, openness, organizational learning and agility.

Keywords: Agility, Authentic Leadership, Collaborative Leadership, Decision Making Science, Group Intelligence, Groupthink, Mental Models, Personal Mastery, Shared Vision, Storytelling, Systems Thinking, Team Learning, Team of Teams.

The role of the 21ˢᵗ century university president is complex and wide-ranging. University presidents are constantly subject to scrutiny. They are held accountable by students and faculty as well as politicians, donors, and the public. They must perform multiple roles: chief academic officer in driving the university's academic agenda; chief operating officer in managing complex campuses with valuable assets; chief marketing officer in terms of the university's reputation and omnipresent social media; chief financial officer in overseeing billion-dollar budgets; and chief fundraiser in cultivating donors. They need financial acumen, business savvy, and political astuteness. They need high-level skills in persuasive communication, strategic management, and entrepreneurship. The pressures of leading a diverse and complex organization, with wide-ranging stakeholders who have divergent aims and world views, are immense. Today's leaders must also possess leadership in technology, since data, analytics and AI are transforming industry, disrupting business models, and providing unprecedented access to the operation of institutions.

The unpredictability of this VUCA (Volatile, Uncertain, Complex and Ambiguous) era, as described in Part II, is fundamentally incompatible with reductionist managerial models based on planning and prediction (McChrystal *et al.* 2015). The new landscape demands a fresh approach, discarding the old management mindset of the last century. Instead, university leaders will need to rely on a network of talents with decentralized decision-making authority, combined with extremely transparent communication. The traditional hierarchy should be replaced with a faster, flatter, more flexible structure. Superficial efficiency and a production-line approach are not enough to survive in this fast-moving world. Leaders should be aware that nothing can be hidden which will not eventually come to light. University leadership is increasingly under the microscope. The only way for a leader to survive is to have a deep sense of his or her true values, and the courage to act on them. Leaders also need to understand their power to allocate resources, and must exercise that power wisely for the good of the institution and society.

To lead effectively in a VUCA world, leaders have to be adaptable to change. The concept of adaptation comes from the process of biological evolution, in which the hardiest organisms are able to survive and thrive in adverse situations (Heifetz, Linsky & Grashow 2009). In times of uncertainty, it is even more crucial for leaders to have strong values and principles. One attribute of effective university presidents is that they are in sync with the DNA of their institutions (Selingo, Chheng & Clark 2017). While the future is unpredictable, leaders learn to read the signs and signals of change, and are receptive to new ideas. They are flexible, knowing how to adjust operational decisions to suit new circumstances while staying true to their mission and values. They are aware that conditions may change, and develop risk management strategies and alternative options to manage uncertainty. Beyond their own inner convictions, leaders need to build institutions which are agile and flexible, which can learn continuously and innovate. They must engage effectively with staff to explain why this culture of flexibility and innovation is critical for institutional survival. More importantly, leaders and their executive team should lead by example.

University leaders have the privilege of leading the world's most elite group of knowledge workers: the faculty. As such, they should avoid crushing academic staff with a set of key performance indicators. Rather, the challenge is to remove obstacles to their performance. Importantly, the idea is not to manage or direct but to influence and inspire (Drucker 1993). To harness the intellectual power of knowledge workers, leaders must be committed to building a supportive culture and effective governance structure. They must develop, motivate and inspire the talent within the university. They need to build trust rather than instil fear. They should provide a nurturing environment where academic staff can flourish in both teaching and research.

According to a large-scale study of 195 leaders of 30 global organizations in 15 countries, Giles (2016) found that the most important competencies valued by leaders are:

- Strong ethics and authenticity
- Empowering others to self-organize
- Fostering a sense of connection and belonging
- Showing openness to new ideas and encouraging organizational learning

These can be crystallized into authenticity, systems thinking, openness, organizational learning and agility: four key concepts for leadership in the VUCA world.

AUTHENTIC LEADERSHIP

Authenticity is a vital leadership characteristic, especially in turbulent and dynamic environments. Leaders operating in challenging circumstances need to create clarity and articulate a strong vision. They need to lead with principle and conviction, in order to guide the organisation forward, fostering its sense of purpose. They need to have empathy and optimism, and exhibit personal courage by taking a stand on critical issues. They need to have passion and the desire to make a difference in the world. They must care deeply about the university's academic mission. . But they must be authentic rather than trying to be someone else. Leaders should act according to their own sense of being, values and beliefs, style and identity. In his book *Authentic Leadership: Rediscovering the Secrets to Creating Lasting Value*, Bill George argues that leaders need to have a genuine sense of themselves. It is much easier to have authenticity in a role when that role aligns with the leader's own beliefs (George 2003). Authentic leaders understand their own purpose and values in life, leading with their hearts while demonstrating self-discipline.

Nelson (2008) has demonstrated the principles of authentic leadership in his case study of three American college and university presidents in New Orleans and the nearby Mississippi coast during the Hurricane Katrina disaster: Dr. Marvelene Hughes at Dillard University, Dr. Norman Christopher Francis at Xavier University of Louisiana, and Dr. Beverly Hogan at Tougaloo College. Nelson describes in vivid detail how these three presidents found themselves in the eye of the storm. Each of them had a deep sense of the purpose of their leadership, and saw themselves as stewards, committed to navigating their institutions into the future.

In times of crisis, what are the authentic values and personal beliefs that these leaders use instinctively to respond to events? Often, initial responses to crises such as Katrina allow no planning at all, and one has to act intuitively when the immediate safety of students and staff are at stake. What is needed is a combination of immense courage, instinct, experience, beliefs, values, and resilience. By taking full control of the situation in assuming command, these three presidents ensured the safety of students and staff.

Moreover, these university leaders displayed outstanding managerial and organizational leadership in the recovery and reconstruction of their universities. Through their collective leadership, they displayed optimism and confidence in rebuilding and re-establishing the functions of the university. They maintained faith with their constituents. Nelson (2008) contends that faith and confidence are key elements in the compass of leadership demonstrated in the case study, embodying the notion of authentic leadership as espoused by Bill George.

SYSTEMS THINKING

Peter Senge, the author of *The Fifth Discipline* who was named as Strategist of the Century by the Journal of Business Strategy, espoused "five component technologies" (disciplines) that converge to support innovation in learning organizations such as universities (Senge 1990). These are: *systems thinking, personal mastery, mental models, building a shared vision, and team learning.*

Systems thinking necessitates a real understanding of process, as opposed to just looking at symptomatic solutions. One must be able to take on multiple perspectives, often examining opposing views to find enduring solutions. Senge's concept of systems thinking shows that there simply is "no right answer" when dealing with complexity. Hence, it is crucial to learn from failures and not be afraid of taking calculated risks, using adversity as opportunities to learn. University leaders must instil this learning culture in their institutions, otherwise there will be a fear of innovation.

Personal mastery means continually clarifying one's personal vision and seeing reality objectively. It is about being in a perpetual learning mode, being acutely aware of one's deficiencies and the need for improvement. Yet it is also about self-confidence and the ability to maintain a creative tension between vision and reality. In understanding self and others, leaders master the concept of *mental models*, which are the deeply ingrained assumptions and generalizations held by individuals. Understanding *mental models* begins with unearthing one's own world views and bringing them to the surface for close scrutiny. This exercise of exposing one's own thinking and making it open to the influence of others allow open dialogue and 'learningful' conversations that balance inquiry and advocacy. This genuine openness will enable the organization to progress and transcend internal politics and game playing.

While it is critical to have a clear vision of the institution to guide judgment, many universities' visions come from the leader or a very small elite group of senior managers who impose their idea of institutional vision on the whole organization. Such top-down visions require compliance not commitment (Senge 1990). A *shared vision* is one to which the people in the organization are committed and which is aligned with their own personal vision. Some failed presidents of universities attributed their demise to their failure of creating a shared vision among their constituents (Paul 2015). The creation of a shared vision requires empathy from leaders to identify with their constituents, understanding their needs and aspirations, their wellbeing and difficulties.

Senge believes that effective *team learning* occurs when the intelligence of the team exceeds the intelligence of the individuals in the team, and where teams develop extraordinary capacities for coordinated action. He extols the virtues of team learning: "when teams are truly learning, not only are they producing extraordinary results but the individual members are growing more rapidly than could have occurred otherwise" (Senge 1990 p10). Furthermore, "a learning team continually fosters other learning teams through inculcating the practices and skills of team learning" (p 237). Central to Senge's team learning is the practice of dialogue (p 237). He explains the difference between dialogue and discussion. Senge cites the physicist Heisenberg's strong belief in the potential of collaborative learning: "that collectively, we can be more insightful, more intelligent than one can possibly be individually". However, Senge pointed out that it is critical to distinguish 'group intelligence' from 'groupthink' – the latter situation is where individuals succumb to group pressure for conformity. In Senge's concept of leadership, the leader is a designer who integrates the ideas of the five disciplines into the purpose, vision and core values for the staff. Leaders are also stewards and teachers, helping their staff develop systemic understanding to ensure sustainability of the organization.

STORYTELLING

Some leadership gurus (John Kotter, Howard Gardner, and Noel Tichy) advocate the use of convincing narrative or storytelling as a leadership tool (Liu 2010). They argue that the storytelling ability is the prerequisite of a winning leader. Leaders should tell stories about themselves, the organization and its aspirations and visions, and how to get to the future. They suggested that CEOs should become Chief Storytelling Officers. In order to run an effective organization, leaders need to provide signals to staff to drive the desired behaviours which are aligned with organizational goals. This applies to the organizational structure, policies and procedures. It also includes the social factors such as organizational ideology, culture, core values, informal networks of communication and influence, leadership style, reward system, and priorities for promotion. Research shows that a successful organization needs more developed people to have long-term organizational success (Liu 2010).

Without the development of the individual, organizational success will be transient. Conversely, only developed individuals without a good support structure will not create a sustainably successful organization. At many universities, outdated management practice still persists in which people are viewed as costs and tools of production. Instead, successful leaders should make staff feel that they are making a valuable contribution to the university and to society. Staff do want to be valued, recognised and rewarded. Therefore, in addition to students, universities should put an emphasis on the development of their staff. If the staff are made to feel that they are cherished, they will behave accordingly and this will result in a better performing organization. Liu (2010) argues that leaders need to treat their employees as people. If you treat employees as a means of production who can be disposed of at any time, they will not behave like people.

COLLABORATIVE LEADERSHIP

Collaborating with others requires an ability to see things from the other side, culturally and professionally. Effective collaboration requires emotional intelligence and insights into one's own capacities and strengths. Silo thinking, attributing blame, overconfidence in one's own abilities, and underrating other people will not be conducive to collaboration. Many institutions ranked leadership as one of the biggest obstacles to effective collaboration. In a connected world, a new concept of leadership is required: one that is more collaborative, tolerant and respectful. Leaders who are open and receptive to new ideas, have the desire to learn, and are respectful of others because of the value they bring (rather than just their positions as staff) will encourage collaboration from the top, inspiring a cooperative atmosphere among teams. Such leaders will set the tone of teamwork and encourages shared decision-making. Collaborative leaders empower their teams to innovate and search for the best solutions. Collaborative leaders will instil a common sense of purpose, building trust and shared values within an institution as well as in a partnership.

DECISION-MAKING SCIENCE

Strong decision-making ability is a key characteristic of successful leaders. But this rather abstract skill, like the getting of wisdom, takes years of experience to perfect. Now, in the 21ˢᵗ century, leaders can benefit from the latest research on decision-making science. This science is based on theories and evidence-based research from psychology, behavioral economics, and neuroscience. It has many tools to help reduce bias and inaccuracies as well as to manage risks. Computer logarithms are improving rapidly at pattern recognition, and machine-learning enables better decision making. Using data analytics, business intelligence, modelling, scenario-generation, machine learning, artificial intelligence and predictive analytics, and data science will help leaders to come to better decisions and produce better business outcomes, augmenting human judgment, intuition and experience. Furthermore, decision-making science helps rational leaders explain their decisions to the organization and the governing board, showing how they reach consistent and transparent decisions, free of emotion or bias. Data science and modelling can be used to test outcomes with sample data, validating and stress-testing before decisions are implemented. These tools can be applied to many aspects of the university, from student recruitment to attracting talented academics.

AGILITY

University leaders are under pressure to innovate and transform their institutions, but it is difficult to turn around these institutions, with their ancient culture, quickly. How to create and instil a culture of innovation and adaptability? Some advice from McKinsey is particularly apt for universities. In the article "Agility: It rhymes with stability" (Aghina, De Smet & Weerda 2015), the authors found from their research that organizations can become more agile and learn to be simultaneously stable and nimble. The secret is in having a stable core or "backbone", which includes the organizational structure, governance, processes, and above all, organizational values. In the case of universities, the academic mission would be the enduring backbone of the institution. Having a stable primary organizational structure gives staff a sense of belonging, even though their daily work and interactions may occur in teams across formal organizational structures. Stability of governance with clear framework is necessary to guide decision-making processes, ensuring that smaller, lower-level decisions occur at the frontline where people have the knowledge and accountability. This frees up university leaders to have the time and energy to focus on the bigger decisions. Flexible, simple and transparent governance structure is critical to the innovative culture of universities. In times of rapid change and uncertainty, it is even more crucial for leaders to have strong values and principles.

Many universities have embarked on a spree of organizational restructures which were later deemed unnecessary and only served to unsettle staff morale and loyalty. Instead, universities should provide a stable and safe organizational environment which allows staff the freedom to experiment and innovate. Academic mission and value are the glue to maintaining stability, while dynamic teams can pursue innovation with speed. In the past, universities adopted a machine view of the organization, with structure following resources, power, and authority in a very precise, methodical way. So every time there is a change, an organizational restructure takes place giving staff a sense of instability and insecurity. Corporate knowledge often vanished with departing staff, while remaining staff were left wondering who would be next. These constant disruptions produce change fatigue in universities, leaving staff disenfranchised and unmotivated to innovate. Major restructure in complex organizations such as universities are to be avoided at all cost. They cause immense disruption and demoralization. Universities are dependent on the commitment and passion of their staff. There are no winners in a restructure, other than those in administrative power who may use it as an opportunity to consolidate their power base.

TEAM OF TEAMS

In this increasingly interdependent and fast-paced world, it is no longer enough to be efficient. In their book *Team of Teams: New Rules of Engagement for a Complex World* (2015), McChrystal *et al.* advocate a new approach. General Stanley McChrystal was the commander of NATO's International Security Assistance Force and all US forces in Afghanistan. When he took command of the Joint Special Operations Task Force in 2004, he quickly realized that conventional military strategies were not working because his opponent was the protean Al Qaeda. To counteract, General McChrystal created adaptable Task Force teams and employed the "command of teams" approach, where relationships between the teams resembled those between individuals on a single team.

There is a need to imbue teams with adaptability and cohesiveness, so that they share common purpose and understanding. Building trust is critical to the effective functioning of teams, and team members need to have open and genuine communications. Such teams will be more adaptable in solving problems and spotting opportunities for innovation. Creating a team of teams fosters cross-silo collaboration. Whether in business or a battlefield, it is critical to be able to react and respond quickly. The "team of teams" approach can be applied to any business or organization. The strategy has been proven to work in a range of workplaces with complex operating environments, from hospital emergency rooms to NASA. University leaders may find it applicable to their senior leadership teams.

CONCLUSION

The most successful presidents have a profound respect and belief in the very idea of the university (Selingo, Chheng & Clark 2017). They will find ways to build long-term sustainability in the institution. Core principles and integrity are the essential ingredients of true leadership. In the university environment, these qualities are particularly critical since universities have a much longer lifespan than companies. University leaders have a duty to preserve the institution for perpetuity. Hence, they should have a long-term perspective and understand the raison d'être of the institution. If leaders do not have strong core values and principles to guide their visions, they will find it difficult to make day-to-day decisions to pursue the academic mission in the best interest of the university. When an environment is volatile and unpredictable, it is even more critical for leaders to have a clear vision and mission focused.

Critically, university leaders need to do a better job of explaining the purpose and value of a university education, otherwise it can only be viewed by society in a superficial way. The primary goal of universities is to educate our next generations and give them the skills and hope on which our future depends. In the words of Dr Paul J. LeBlanc, president of Southern New Hampshire University, at the American Council on Education's 100th Annual Meeting in March 2018:

"Our future hinges on whether we have ambitious, socially connected, networked, savvy kids who have hope or who are hopeless. Because, it's in their hopelessness that breeds the roots of civil discontent and discord that we see in so many parts of the world. When we give them education and tools to better their lives, we are in the business of hope and we are in the business of making the future better …….. higher education is the engine of social mobility and the engine of social justice. And, that's what we do every day collectively" (Chatlani 2018b).

CHAPTER 28

Leadership Challenge in the Case of the University of Hong Kong

Abstract: This section examines leadership challenges in the case of the University of Hong Kong. Since the handover of the former British colony to the People's Republic of China in 1997, Hong Kong has been governed as a Special Administrative Region (SAR) under the "One Country-Two Systems" policy, able to maintain political-economic autonomy from the Chinese mainland. While Hong Kong enjoys the greatest degree of freedom of any city in China, its citizens are worried that this freedom could be eroded with mainland China's rising influence. The Occupy Central movement, which originated in 2011, evolved into a movement to Occupy Central with Love and Peace by 2013. Its aim was to promote peaceful civil disobedience and protests, with the goal of persuading Beijing to allow Hong Kong to have what they consider as genuine universal suffrage in the election of the City's Chief Executive.

The University of Hong Kong, as the city's oldest and largest higher education institution and symbolic of the colonial past, was on a political knife-edge. Some of the University staff and students were deeply involved in the Occupy Central with Love and Peace movement. At the same time, the University was experiencing low morale as result of recent changes in governance and management reforms. The University has been transitioning from a collegiate to a corporate model of governance structure, a move which has not been completely embraced by the faculty. Universities in Hong Kong are reviewing their governance structure, since the Chancellor of each university is by default the Chief Executive of the Government of Hong Kong (formerly the Governor of Hong Kong prior to 1997). There have been calls by critics and student bodies to remove the Chief Executive as the Chancellor of the universities. It is in this climate that Professor Peter Mathieson was hired as the University's new Vice-Chancellor. Mathieson was the first British Vice-Chancellor recruited directly from England since Dr Kenneth Ernest Robinson's time as the University's ninth Vice-Chancellor (1965 – 1972). Initially, his appointment was greeted with open cynicism from the University's community. However, the following chapter analyzes the change in community opinion, as Mathieson showed extraordinary leadership in guiding the University through a complex and delicate situation. Mathieson's strong principles and close adherence to the fundamentals of the academic mission have stood him well. The chapter begins with an explanation of the governance issues in Hong Kong universities, the Occupy Hong Kong movement, and finally, the leadership of Professor Mathieson. The analysis was based on newspaper articles, videos and meetings with Professor Mathieson.

Keywords: Academic Freedom, Academic Mission, Authentic Leadership, General Education, Governance Reforms, Hong Kong universities, Occupy Hong Kong.

INTRODUCTION

Hong Kong, a coastal island located off the southern coast of China and a former British colony since 1841, was reunited with mainland China in 1997. It is now a Special Administrative Region (SAR) under the "One Country-Two Systems" policy, able to maintain political-economic autonomy from mainland China. With the end of British rule, Hong Kong took the opportunity to reform its Higher Education which was previously based on the British model of specialization (Jaffee 2013).

As a result, universities in Hong Kong have adopted a four-year undergraduate degree (University Grants Committee 2002) with a common first year, in the tradition of US universities such as Harvard and University of California Berkeley. The purpose of this change is to enrich the preparation of Hong Kong graduates with a liberal arts education through a broader knowledge base and whole-person development. On a broader level, the aim is to support the transition of Hong Kong's economy from a manufacturing to a service- and knowledge-based economy, driven by knowledge workers with diverse and adaptable skills.

Hong Kong has twenty degree-awarding higher education institutions, including eight universities funded by the Government through the University Grants Committee, eleven self-financing institutions and a publicly funded institution. The eight universities receive funding from the Hong Kong Government *via* the University Grants Committee (UGC) of Hong Kong, which acts as an independent expert advisor to the Government (Hong Kong Education Bureau) on the development and funding needs of the universities. Hong Kong has a well-differentiated higher education system, with each institution having its own unique strengths and niche focus. The UGC ensures that mechanisms are in place to incentivize institutions to maintain clear role differentiation, while also enabling deep collaboration and constructive competition between institutions. As a result, Hong Kong has a high-performing higher education system, with a number of highly-ranked universities. The differentiated system is much admired in the international community (Davis 2017).

GOVERNANCE ISSUES IN HONG KONG UNIVERSITIES

All universities in Hong Kong have been incorporated under the Ordinances of the Hong Kong Government, which define the University's powers and duties, privileges, and constitutions, as well as the University's office bearers. The

Chancellor of each university is the Chief Executive of the Government of Hong Kong (formerly the Governor of Hong Kong prior to 1997), who has the power to appoint a substantial number of the university Council members, including the chair, deputy chair and treasurer.

THE SUTHERLAND REVIEW

Since the British handover in 1997, there have been several controversial incidents which raised concerns over the changing government-university relationship in Hong Kong (Lee 2014). In 2002, the University Grants Committee commissioned a review of Hong Kong's Higher Education system, which was led by Lord Sutherland. Subsequently, the University Grants Committee and the Hong Kong Government adopted the recommendations of the Sutherland Report on the future development of Higher Education in Hong Kong, including the recommendation that:

"the governing body of each university carry out a review of the fitness for purpose of its governance and management structures. Such an exercise will necessarily include a review of the relevant Ordinances and, where appropriate, proposals for legislative changes should be made."

Recommendation 6, Sutherland Report 2002

In 2013, following the completion of the structural reviews of each university, the Hong Kong Education Bureau requested the UGC to do a follow-up study on the governance of the universities, to benchmark against the best practice of other international institutions. The study was led by Sir Howard Newby. The 2015 Newby Report outlines the key issues for universities to consider when determining any changes to their governance structure. It provides some comparative information on the university governance structure in the UK, USA, Australia, Canada, New Zealand and Singapore. It offers specific recommendations on matters such as: the identification of candidates for membership of the university council and their continuing professional development; fiduciary responsibilities of council members having to strike an appropriate balance between institutional autonomy and public accountability; a set of key performance indicators to be incorporated in each university's strategic plan to facilitate council members to assess progress; a risk management plan for major institutional risks including financial and reputational risks; a clear framework for delegation of authority; and regular reviews of university governance by UGC.

However, the Report was silent on any changes to the university Ordinances. It did nonetheless identify the problems in the process by which Council members were appointed.

"The Chief Executive, in his role as Chancellor of the universities, appoints a significant proportion of council members, although the exact number and proportion varies from one university to another. In addition, some universities, by virtue of their history, have reserved places for members of their founding charities or foundations. This situation contrasts with most other countries whereby councils themselves are responsible for appointing their own members, creating a nominations committee to undertake this task".

Newby Report 2015 page 20

The report went on to state that:

"in order to maintain public confidence in the governance of universities, it is important that their governing bodies are broadly reflective of the stakeholders which have a legitimate interest in their affairs".

Newby Report 2015 page 20

Despite calls for the removal of the Chief Executive of the Hong Kong Government as the Chancellor of the universities by some critics and student bodies, no change was made to the Ordinance when the former Hong Kong Institute of Education was made a full university in May 2016. It states under Section 6 of the Ordinance that *"The Chief Executive shall be the Chancellor of the University"*. A number of universities in Hong Kong, including the University of Hong Kong, Chinese University of Hong Kong, and Hong Kong Baptist University, have recently set up mechanisms to review their university governance structures in response to community concerns.

OCCUPY HONG KONG

Hong Kong adopted the international "Occupy" protest movement against social and economic inequality between October 2011 to September 2012, representing one of the longest Occupy movements in the world. The movement was a reaction to the consequences of globalization and the fallout from the Global Financial Crisis of 2008. The Occupy Hong Kong movement was re-ignited in late 2013, with a view to pursuing universal suffrage in the election of the Hong Kong Chief Executive in 2017. Some of the staff and students of University of Hong Kong (HKU) were deeply involved in the movement, leading to the accusation that the subsequent non-appointment of one of its members to the University's leadership position was due to political interference by the Chief Executive of the Hong Kong Government. This, in turn, sparked off more protests from the staff and students of HKU against the perceived meddling by Government in academic freedom and institutional autonomy, calling for the immediate removal of the Chief Executive of Hong Kong as chancellor of universities in Hong Kong.

One of the Occupy Hong Kong movement's prominent campaigners was Benny Tai Yiuting, Associate Professor of Law at the University of Hong Kong, who advocated the Occupy Central with Love and Peace (OCLP). In 2014, OCLP organised a civic referendum on the voting system to be used for the election of the chief executive in 2017. The Civic Referendum involved the OCLP commissioning the University of Hong Kong Public Opinion Programme (HKUPOP) to run a poll, calling for the public to be allowed to nominate candidates for the 2017 chief executive election. It would appear that Occupy Central represents a protest for universal suffrage as part of Hong Kong's struggle for electoral democracy. However, there has been conjecture that the underlying reason is a deeper dissatisfaction with income inequality in Hong Kong (Chen 2014). The Gini coefficient for Hong Kong reached 0.537 in 2011, up 25% from 0.45 in 1981. Hong Kong's exorbitant housing prices are higher than those of New York and London. Young people feel economically disenfranchised by a system they blame for leaving a generation locked out of the housing market and making an already troubling income divide even worse. The City's wealth is concentrated in the top 1% of the population, and the growing economic reliance on China is causing concerns in the Hong Kong people who are experiencing hardship in a low economic growth environment (Noble 2014).

However, university students in Hong Kong are not alone in this plight. Income inequality is continuing to spread internationally. A recent report by McKinsey, *"Poorer Than Their Parents? Flat or Falling Incomes in Advanced Economies"* (Dobbs *et al.* 2016), has found that the trend of stagnating or declining incomes for middle class workers is a global phenomenon, affecting workers across the developed world. The McKinsey researchers linked income inequality to the high levels of social and political instability in both advanced and developing economies. At a time when other countries such as the UK, USA and Australia are debating cutting public funding to their universities, the universities in Hong Kong are receiving adequate funding from their government. In fact, university students in HKU are enjoying one of the best university education Asia could offer. The majority of university students in the West have to pay much higher fees and incur huge personal debts, while their graduate employment outlook is much dimmer than the situation in Hong Kong. Graduate unemployment is as high as 7.2% in the US, 11.3% in Australia and 13% in UK, while HKU students enjoy a 99.7% employment rate.

It should be noted that there is a growing international trend of anti-establishment sentiments which are being reflected in the Hong Kong society, suggesting that there are some deeper societal and economic problems. Many citizens are angry about falling wages, unaffordable house prices, high cost of living, income inequality, and most importantly, social immobility for young people. Resentment is often directed at those in charge, the so-called 'elites' who have been running the show. The sense that there is a lack of leadership to tackle social problems has been demonstrated around the world such as those in the 2016 Brexit campaign, where British voters decided to reject the establishment and vote to leave the European Union. Similarly, in the 2016 US Presidential Election, supporters were attracted to Donald Trump's anti-establishment rhetoric. In Australia, these sentiments manifested themselves in the election of many minor political parties instead of the two major parties. In Hong Kong, the Occupy Hong Kong movement and events happening in the universities became a lightning rod for young people to vent their frustration and anger.

THE UNIVERSITY OF HONG KONG (HKU)

Of the eight universities funded by the University Grants Committee (UGC), the University of Hong Kong is the oldest and largest tertiary institution in Hong Kong. It was founded in 1911 by the then Governor of Hong Kong, Sir Frederick Lugard. The University was established as a self-governing body of scholars by a University Ordinance on March 30, 1911. In actual fact, its Faculty of Medicine had evolved from the Hong Kong College of Medicine, originally founded in 1887 where Dr. Sun Yat-sen was one of its first students.

The University is a comprehensive research university with ten faculties (Architecture, Arts, Education, Engineering, Law, Science, Social Sciences, Business and Economics, Dentistry and Medicine), one Graduate School, and 88 research centres and institutes. It enjoys a high world ranking in spite of the previous criticisms levelled at the University. In 2017/18, the University experienced a turnaround in its position in the three major international league tables. The University is currently ranked 26ᵗʰ in the QS World University rankings, 40ᵗʰ in Times Higher Education World Reputation University Rankings, and 101-150ᵗʰ in the Academic Ranking of World Universities – the highest ranking achieved by the University since the inception of the Academic Ranking of World Universities in 2003. Remarkably, the University's graduates have achieved an almost full employment rate of 99.7% for the past six years, a situation which is the envy of many international universities. In fact, a recent global graduate salaries survey found that the starting salaries of Hong Kong graduates are the highest in the world among the countries surveyed (Times Higher Education World Reputation University Rankings 2016).

HKU GOVERNANCE REVIEWS

After UGC's 2002 Sutherland Report which recommended a review of the fitness for purpose of all Hong Kong universities' governance and management structures, HKU was the first UGC-funded university to undergo a governance review in 2003. The review was led by Professor John Niland, former Vice-Chancellor and President of the University of New South Wales, Australia, Professor Neil L Rudenstine, the 26th President of Harvard University and the Hon Chief Justice Andrew K N Li, Head of the Judiciary of the Hong Kong Special Administrative Region.

The 2003 Fit for Purpose Report made 17 recommendations across a number of issues, but its major focus was on maintaining a distinction between governance and management, as well as supporting a devolved executive management. One of the most significant recommendations was that the faculty deans would no longer be elected by academic staff. Instead they would be appointed by senior management on the recommendation of the Vice-Chancellor.

R11. Deans of Faculties should all be appointed, by the Council on the recommendation of the Vice-Chancellor, as full-time officers on five-year terms through a transparent due process, with international search.

The Report also recommended that while students could be elected to the University Council, they must adhere to the strict rules of confidentiality and not be simultaneously holding office in the Students' Union. It is worth noting that Professor Niland had extensive experience in both university leadership and staff association of universities, having been a National President of the Federation of Australian University Staff Associations and President of the Australian Vice-Chancellor's Committee. His professional qualifications include Fellowships of the Academy of Social Sciences in Australia and the Australian Institute of Company Directors. In the Report, Professor Niland clearly applied the sound principles of the Australian system of corporate governance to his recommendations.

As a comparison, it is worthwhile to note that in Australia, the Australian Government has set a limit to the size of university councils (22), recommending the removal of student and academic staff representation on governing councils, and that external members should constitute the majority of the governing body (Australian Parliamentary Inquiry into the Higher Education Legislation Amendment Bill (No.3) 2004 - Chapter 3 - University Governance and management issues). The reason for this move was that the Australian Government had shifted its public universities from a primarily government-funded model towards a 'user-pays' system. The Government has defined universities as providers of educational services and used the revised legislation as a way to support "the transformation of universities from what they see to be cloistered institutions towards a more entrepreneurial role" (section 23. 23). As such, the Australian Government reasoned that a more entrepreneurial approach to financial management required a different imprint of corporate governance and that the membership of the governing bodies should be made on the basis of their skills and abilities to contribute to the governance of the universities. It was felt that some of the former members (academic and student representatives) regarded themselves as representing the interests of their particular constituencies rather than acting as part of the collective leadership of the university.

On the issue of government representation on universities' governing bodies, some of the Australian states have abolished parliamentary representation on university governing bodies (Australian Parliamentary 2004). However, in the state of New South Wales, there is still strong support for the continuation of parliamentary representation on universities' governing bodies. In fact, some universities have found it useful to have a suitable parliamentarian on their governing bodies (section 23.42). Despite the fact that the Government does not favour the appointment of parliamentary representatives on university governing bodies (section 23.43), it still appoints varying numbers of members to the university councils *via* the state education ministers and Governors-in-Council. This is quite a contrast to the situation in Hong Kong, where considerable numbers of students and staff members have objected violently to any government participation in the universities' governing councils. It is useful to note that the question of the Chief Executive of the Government (or the Governor prior to 1997) being the Chancellor of Hong Kong universities has not raised significant concerns until now. It is true that having the Chief Executive of Hong Kong Government in this role is unconventional in the modern era. On the other hand, there is a potential benefit in having an assurance of support to universities at the highest level of government. Can universities ever have real autonomy? The reality is that they always have to be mindful of the needs of their funding masters. While most higher education systems in the West appear to have a high level of institutional autonomy, their governments do closely steer their universities through funding allocations and research priorities, all in the name of accountability. While governments declare their commitment to upholding the values of academic freedom, they direct universities through various forms of regulation and politically-determined imperatives. In reality, politics is an inescapable consideration for most Western universities.

In 2009, the University of Hong Kong conducted a Five Year Review led by Professor Niland to assess the progress made since the 2003 Report in terms of the transformation the University had made in its structures and processes. The review found that the majority of the recommendations had been fully implemented, with the exception of three areas. One area in which the recommendation was not followed concerned the adoption of the trusteeship principle: the recommendation was to have no office holders of staff or student associations among the University Council membership (Niland Report 2009). Following the refusal by the then Chairman of the Academic Staff Association and the President of HKU Student Union (both elected Council members) to resign as office bearers from their respective bodies, the Council resolved that office bearers of staff and student associations who were elected to the Council could continue to serve on the University Council provided that they guarantee in writing that they would serve on the Council and discharge their role as Council members in a personal capacity, not necessarily adhering to the stance taken by their associations (page 11 Niland Review 2009).

In October 2012, the Standing Committee HKU Convocation produced a Report on the Future of the University of Hong Kong. It made major recommendations on the University's core values, recommending improvements in its governance and management structures by adapting and combining the best of the corporate and the collegial model of shared governance. It also recommended that the University conduct regular reviews of its mission and strategy to meet the changing needs of the globalised world; uphold the importance of liberal education; pursue excellence in research as well as in undergraduate teaching; formulate a strategy on effective engagement with China; and develop an effective and sustainable strategy to engage and support alumni development. In Section 53 of the Report, it pointed out that both the Deputy Vice-Chancellor and the Pro-Vice-Chancellor positions should be filled on a merit basis through an international search process, and that the whole University must embrace the appointed Deanship as the norm. This recommendation, together with those contained in the Niland reports (2003 and 2009), are significant. While the University is transitioning from a collegiate to a corporate model of governance structure, the latter is not fully embraced by the faculty. This continues to be a source of discontent in the academic community.

In October 2011, the then Vice-Chancellor Professor Tsui Lap-Chee decided not to seek re-appointment at the end of his contract in August 2012, after 12 years' service. Professor Tsui had been a very successful Vice-Chancellor and a formidable fundraiser for the University. However, during his tenure, there was an unfortunate incident: the so-called Hong Kong 818 incident, which occurred during the Chinese Vice-Premier's visit to the University. According to a subsequent report, the HK police was accused of using unnecessary force towards the students in locked-down parts of the University campus. Professor Tsui later apologised to the University community for allowing such an incident to take place (Chou 2014). In October 2013, the University of Hong Kong officially appointed its first non-Chinese expatriate chief in a decade. In fact, Professor Peter Mathieson is the first Briton recruited directly from England since Dr Kenneth Ernest Robinson was the University's ninth Vice-Chancellor (1965 – 1972).

Peter Mathieson, a distinguished renal physician and former Dean of Faculty of Medicine & Dentistry at the University of Bristol, United Kingdom, was not a total stranger to Hong Kong, having been an Overseas Examiner in Medicine for the Chinese University of Hong Kong. While he had been invited to be a member of the Health Sciences Panel in the 2014 Research Assessment Exercise (RAE) by the University Grants Committee of Hong Kong, he immediately resigned from the role as soon as he was appointed as Vice-Chancellor of HKU and did not participate in the RAE process. In announcing the appointment, the University Council Chairman Dr Leong Che-hung informed the media that Professor Mathieson was the only candidate shortlisted for the position, and received "unanimous" blessing from the HKU Council. Dr Leong described Professor Mathieson as having excellent academic standing, integrity, vision, management capability, and communication skills for this important position. Nevertheless, there were open criticisms levelled at Professor Mathieson's lack of experience in Hong Kong and China.

LEADERSHIP CHALLENGE

Professor Peter Mathieson was the fifteenth President and Vice-Chancellor of the University of Hong Kong, and assumed office on 1st April 2014. He arrived at a time when HKU was experiencing low morale after staff policy changes including forced retirements and reduction of staff benefits, and seemingly inadequate research funding. The University was also transitioning from a collegiate to a corporate model of governance and management structure, which was not completely embraced by the faculty. It is understandable that the appointment of an outsider from Britain as the new Vice-Chancellor would not have been well received. Responding to the criticism about his lack of experience in Hong Kong and China, Professor Mathieson said that he saw it as an advantage because he would be able to "start afresh with no predefined standpoint or baggage" (SCMP 2013). It is true that given Hong Kong's delicate political situation, a person from outside the region could prove useful in providing academic and impartial leadership for the University.

Born in the UK and educated at the University of London and University of Cambridge, Mathieson was the youngest President ever elected (in 2007) to the Renal Association UK. Since 2008, he was Dean of the Faculty of Medicine &

Dentistry and Professor of Medicine at the University of Bristol. He was for many years a member of the International Society of Nephrology (ISN) and of its committee for Africa. He participated in many of the ISN visits to East Africa and has been a regular contributor to the medical education in that region.

When the announcement of Professor Mathieson's appointment as the Vice-Chancellor of the University of Hong Kong was first made in October 2013, the news was greeted with open cynicism and belligerence, with critics questioning his academic achievements, background and vision. Little did the HKU community know that he would turn out to be one of its most caring vice-chancellors of the University. Professor Mathieson's strong principles and close adherence to the fundamentals of academic mission have stood him well. His calm and unflustered spirit has won him admiration from the Hong Kong community. While his appointment initially met with unwelcoming remarks, he seemed to have taken these on board philosophically. He had evidently studied the history and background of Hong Kong, since he demonstrated real understanding and insight into the political situation. His unswerving defence of the University had won over many of its staff and students. He had strong academic principles and vowed to protect academic freedom. He supported students' right to peaceful protest and free expression. Professor Mathieson demonstrated authentic and exemplary leadership in guiding the University through the most complex and turbulent times since its inception.

AUTHENTIC LEADERSHIP

Authenticity is a vital leadership characteristic, especially in a turbulent and dynamic environment (PWC Leadership for the Future 2008). Leaders operating in challenging circumstances need to create clarity and articulate a clear vision. They need to lead with principles and conviction in order to guide the organisation forward, fostering its sense of purpose. They need to have empathy and optimism, and exhibit personal courage by taking a stand on critical issues. The role of a university vice-chancellor is extremely demanding and the difficulties of leading a diverse and complex organisation made up of constituents with divergent worldviews and objectives are immense. The author once spoke to a former CEO of a large international banking corporation, who later took on the position of Chancellor at a large Australian university. When asked about the differences he found between the two organisations, he said that leading a university was far more difficult than leading a multinational bank. For a university, the internal stakeholders were so much more diverse, including professors, academics, administrators, students, alumni and university council members. In addition, there were external stakeholders such as the communities, industries, state and federal governments, donors. The interests of all these parties were not necessarily in agreement.

Authentic leaders have a passion and care deeply about their ideals. They act according to their own values and beliefs, and their own identities (George 2003, Nelson 2008). They demonstrate a deep understanding of their purpose, practice solid values, and exercise self-discipline in the most trying situations. The following examples illustrate the authentic leadership of Professor Mathieson.

CONNECTING WITH STUDENTS

A truly authentic leader has a deep sense of empathy for others. Mathieson understood his students and put their and the University's interests first. He staunchly maintained that his priority was to take care of the students of HKU, comparing himself to be a "quasi-parent" of some 28,000 students – and his role was to guide them rather than dictate to them. He enjoyed participating in student activities and often shared some of his personal experiences with students. He told students about his childhood, moving around the UK due to his father's job in the Merchant Navy, and being brought up by his mother after his father's death. He wanted students to be able to identify with him and not regard him as aloof or inaccessible. He often welcomed the students by speaking in Chinese, and even took "selfies" with them (Girls4Tech 2016).

A CARING VICE-CHANCELLOR

How many vice-chancellors would leave their house in the middle of the night to talk to student protestors? Within months of Professor Mathieson's arrival, the Occupy Central protests re-ignited in Hong Kong. On the night of 2ⁿᵈ October 2014, crowds of student protestors went to the Hong Kong Chief Executive's office in Tamar, Admiralty, demanding the resignation of the incumbent. On that day, Mathieson had been in regular communication with the students, and it was clear to him that the situation was deteriorating. At around 10 pm, he asked the President of the Student Union Yvonne Leung whether it would help if he went down to Tamar. When Leung said that it would, Professor Mathieson immediately asked the Chinese University of HK's Vice-Chancellor Professor Joseph Sung to join him (they knew each other from the days when Professor Mathieson was an external examiner at CUHK). He later realised that it was an emotive reaction, not one that was carefully thought through, but he felt it was the right thing to do at the time. In hindsight, he realised that it was actually a rather risky action. On arriving at the protest site, the students formed a cordon around the two vice-chancellors, allowing them to pass through the dense crowd. The students kept cheering, clapping and chanting "Vice-Chancellor, Vice-Chancellor" in Cantonese. When asked by the journalists how he felt on being cheered by the students, Mathieson said that he felt embarrassed. That day was dubbed "Wet

Shirt Day" as it was an extremely hot night and Mathieson was drenched in sweat. He climbed onto a ladder and urged students to "put safety first" and "avoid conflict". He appealed to the students to have peaceful protests to allow dialogue and proceed towards reconciliation. While this did not make the problems disappear, it took the edge off the crisis. The visit gave the protestors a sense that they were being heard: that their vice-chancellors cared about them enough to come out in the middle of the night to talk to them. The students finally disbanded, with a promise from the Chief Executive to have a dialogue with the student leaders. Professor Mathieson felt that it was a defining moment of his presidency and that he had contributed to preventing further escalation of the student protest.

STRONG ON PRINCIPLES

Authentic leaders are mission-focussed and interested in genuine outcomes rather than spin. They have strong internalised moral values and integrity. In this regard, Mathieson's leadership was unspoiled by ego and rhetoric. When HKU was ranked 3ʳᵈ in the list of the most *international* universities in the world in 2016 (it was ranked 52ⁿᵈ in 2015) in the Times Higher Education World University Rankings, he wrote in an article in the Times Higher Education cautioning against overreliance on the outcomes of league tables in setting university policies. He went on to explain that he could not take credit for the meteoric rise of HKU's ranking, attributing it instead to a methodological change in counting China as "international" in relation to Hong Kong. He also warned against complacency when the University's ranking was high. Instead, one should continue to strive for excellence in the University's missions (Mathieson 2016 Times Higher Education p 39). He said that universities should work with the ranking agencies to improve and enhance ranking methodologies in order to make them more reliable, credible and accurate.

Similarly, in the QS ranking, despite HKU's position had dropped a few notches in recent years, it still ranks second in the Asian University Rankings, with its Dentistry discipline being ranked first. Nevertheless, Mathieson argued against putting too much emphasis on university rankings and stressed that they should not dictate university policy. Instead, "we have to aspire to excellence in everything we do," he said in an interview with the Financial Times (Paleit 2014). He asserted that the University will pursue its academic aspirations and visions in the best interests of the University and will not be swayed by the fickleness of various rankings. It is inspirational to hear a vice-chancellor being so grounded. This is in stark contrast to the author's previous findings on Australian universities, where a substantial number of Australian universities mentioned high rankings as one of their major goals in their mission statements (Chow 2013). In

your online bookshop

Order date:	13/02/2019
Order reference:	AUK-46023309
Dispatch note:	20190215132001

Your Order

ISBN	Title	Quantity
9781681087504	Redefining University Leadership for ...	1

For returns information visit wordery.com/returns. Please keep this receipt for your records.

Thank you for your Wordery order. We hope you enjoy your book #HappyReading

your online bookshop

20190215132001

fact, many universities in the UK, USA, Australia and Europe regard ranking and internationalisation as a means to boost their reputation, and attract more international students who bring in additional revenues.

Mathieson demonstrated a real understanding of university systems. Instead of simply extolling the rhetoric and virtues of internationalisation, he explained that many universities in the West use internationalisation for revenue-raising. This is particularly the case in the UK and Australia, where international students contribute significantly to the countries' economies. According to University UK, British universities derive one-seventh of their income from international students' tuition fees, and these students contribute around £25.8 billion to the economy in 2014-15. This is in addition to the 700,000 plus students studying transnational programs of UK universities offshore. In Australia, international education is the country's largest services export, valued at over $28 billion in 2016-17 and contributing on average one-quarter of total university revenue. A few Australian universities have over 40% in international student enrolments (Australian Bureau of Statistic, Ross & Hare 2016).

In Hong Kong, the Government sets a quota of 20% for international undergraduate student enrolments in publicly funded universities. In HKU, internationalisation is genuinely about having a diversity of student body and welcoming students from all over the world, from Africa to China. Professor Mathieson expressed pride in the diversity of HKU students and was delighted to hear so many languages being spoken around the campus, enhancing the richness of the University environment. He also paid tribute to the international students' proficiency in English, being the common language for communication in an international community.

A DOSE OF POLITICAL REALISM

The appointment of the first vice-chancellor from Britain since 1972 must seem to reflect the legacy of a bygone era. Yet Mathieson demonstrated a real understanding of the political realities of Hong Kong's position. While he fully appreciated the quandary that Hong Kong was in, he insisted that Hong Kong is now part of China and will be increasingly so in the decades to come. He observed that the recent student protests and calls for self-determination and independence were a symptom and not the disease. It was a way by which the students expressed their frustration at not being able to master their destinies and determine their own future. Their desperation was manifested in a call for independence which was absolutely unrealistic and improbable. Coming from a British Vice-Chancellor, such an assertion definitely sounds more convincing. Mathieson tirelessly reminded his staff and students that Hong Kong has a superior and well-funded Higher Education system which is the envy of the world. The University should seize the opportunities offered by Hong Kong's special relationship with mainland China, and not be distracted by current politics.

In the past, HKU had only limited formal collaboration with institutions in China relative to top Western universities such as Duke or Johns Hopkins or other Hong Kong universities such as Chinese University of Hong Kong and Baptist University. One of its collaborations was a joint MBA with Fudan University, which was launched in 1998. Mathieson continued the good work begun by former Vice-Chancellor Professor Tsui. He was strongly committed to the University of Hong Kong Zhejiang Institute of Research and Innovation (HKU-ZIRI). The HKU-ZIRI provides research and development in high-end and cutting-edge disciplines in three main research laboratories: Industrial Internet-of-Things, Nanofluids and Thermal Engineering, and Aerodynamics and Acoustics.

Professor Mathieson also reaffirmed a strong commitment to HKU's project in Shenzhen, where HKU had built a hospital despite some controversy over the finances of the operation. He and his team had since improved the financial position of the Hospital, having reached an agreement with the Hospital management on a detailed repayment schedule for the services provided by HKU staff. There is now a greater understating between the partners with regard to their respective interests and needs, with improved communication between the parties and joint efforts in in running and planning for the Hospital. The Hospital has also begun to focus on research and teaching as a public teaching tertiary hospital should. Mathieson always recognised the benefits of having a teaching and research hospital across the border in the booming metropolis of Shenzhen. With his extensive experience in collaborating between a university and a healthcare system in UK, he was instrumental in restoring the good relationship with the Shenzhen Government. Now HKU's medical, nursing and Chinese Medicine students and other researchers have access to the unique patient population and research materials, as well as grants from the region. The Hospital will also be able to contribute to the healthcare reform in Mainland China. Its outpatient treatment regimens and booking systems are now being copied in other local hospitals resulting in a reduction in the length of hospital stays and the use of antibiotics.

Mathieson devoted a great deal of his time to this project and made many visits to the Hospital, tracking its progress closely. At the 2016 opening of Shenzhen's first children's dialysis centre, the Shenzhen Children's Hospital Dialysis Centre and Paediatric Intensive Care Unit, Professor Mathieson expressed great pleasure in seeing the success achieved by the Hospital: "I reiterate my pride in HKU's continued commitments to the hospital" (Liu 2016). Since its establishment four years ago, the HKU-SZ Hospital has been hailed as a pilot for introducing medical reforms in China. In January 2014, the Hospital became the first in China to have obtained The Australian Council on Healthcare Standards (ACHS) Certification, and in September 2015 it received full accreditation status for a four-year period. Mathieson tirelessly repeated his message that the University has to overcome any political challenges concerning the relationship with the mainland, as the China relationship is very important to the University and it is an area which the University needs to further develop.

COURAGE AND INTEGRITY

Authentic leaders have the fortitude and courage to do the right thing in the face of adversity. They are mission-driven, able to put the mission and goals of the organization ahead of their own self-interest. In this regard, Mathieson was not fearful of, or fazed by his critics, since he had a very simple principle: that is, to do what is best for the University and not be distracted by the politics. He had won over many of his critics due to his rational approach to solving problems. Most importantly, Mathieson had a deep sense of conviction in the pursuit of the University's academic mission. He steadfastly maintained the neutrality of the University's position in relation to Hong Kong's politics. He valued comments from the community, preferring to work for a university which attracts a great deal of interest from the community rather than for one that no-one cares about. In his own words:

"Even if this undue focus brings pressures and complexities, we should welcome it, embrace it and use it to our advantage. We have plenty of ammunition with which to defend ourselves, plenty of evidence of the University's excellence and its maintenance of standards".

Professor Mathieson's speech at the HKU Court meeting
December 15, 2016

ON ACADEMIC FREEDOM

Mathieson staunchly defended academic freedom and the right of free expression. He quoted the Stone Report of the University of Chicago on Freedom of Expression, which is widely adopted by many US universities such as Purdue, Princeton, American University, Johns Hopkins, and the University of Wisconsin (Economist 2016). In brief, the Stone Report states that the university encourages constructive criticism provided such expression would not violate the law, falsely defame or constitute a genuine threat or harassment, or impede the functioning of the university (Report of the Committee on Freedom of Expression at the University of Chicago). However, it is important to note that academic freedom is confined only to academic commitment in the pursuit of knowledge and the performance of academic duties in the course of teaching and research. The freedom is not absolute, but guided by an implicit code of conduct which includes integrity, honesty, neutrality and testifiability (Macintyre 2010; Nelson 2010). Unfortunately, the limited scope of the academic freedom is not fully understood by many of the academic community. On 15 September 2017, the ten heads of universities in Hong Kong issued a public statement that

"We treasure freedom of expression, but we condemn its recent abuses. Freedom of expression is not absolute, and like all freedoms it comes with responsibilities. All universities undersigned agree that we do not support Hong Kong independence, which contravenes the Basic Law".

Chinese University of Hong Kong (CUHK)
Communications and Public Relations Office

IMPROVING ACCESS

Access to and participation in higher education for disadvantaged students should be part of every university's academic mission. Yet in practice, university admission policies based on meritocracy tend to favour socially privileged groups (Horne & Sherington 2010). As a transformational leader, Mathieson wanted HKU to aspire to the ideal of the academic mission - to provide greater access to students from low socio-economic backgrounds in Hong Kong. He personally had made visits to schools in low socio-economic areas such as Tuen Mun and talked to students there in order to inspire them to aspire to go to HKU. He did recognise that these students' lesser English-language skills could be a barrier, but he was willing to consider lowering the entry criteria for these disadvantaged students and providing them with some form of pre-university support to bring them up to the required level. When so many universities in the UK and Australia are accused of not making a concerted effort to improve access to students from low socio-economic backgrounds, it is inspiring to have the vice-chancellor of the most elite university in Hong Kong go out and talk to the disadvantaged youths. In addition, HKU has now set up the *First-in-the-Family Education Fund* to support students who are the first generation in their families to attend university to participate in outside-classroom learning activities. The aim is to enable students from low socio-economic families to fully participate in their studies without financial constraints.

FOLLOWING THE LOCAL TRADITIONS

Authentic leaders continuously learn from, and adapting to the environment. Mathieson demonstrated genuine respect for Hong Kong's local culture and history. Prior to his arrival, Mathieson undertook lessons in Cantonese with the help of a Malaysian teacher. On his first day on the job, he was able to surprise the audience by greeting them in Cantonese (albeit with a Malaysian accent), which was reported by the South China Morning Post that "Mathieson, who surprised an audience with greetings in fluent Cantonese...." (Zhao 2014). And during the Lunar New Year of the Lamb, Mathieson and his family went to visit villages in the New Territories and participated in some of the local festive events. He wished everybody Happy Chinese New Year in fluent Cantonese and was able to write the Chinese character for "lamb" with a calligraphy brush!

AUTHENTIC STUDENT EXPERIENCE

Mathieson spoke highly of HK's higher education system being well-funded by its Government, in contrast to many international systems which are oriented towards a user-pay model. For example, the UK is headed towards the fee-paying system of the US. UK students have to pay tuition fees of £9,250 pa, one of the highest in OECD countries. HK students might be worried about political interference and the fact that the Government is taking an interest in its Higher Education system, but international universities are not free from these problems. While UK universities pride themselves as having institutional autonomy, government interference does exist, albeit in different forms. In the West, governments closely steer universities through market competition, compliance regulation and output-based funding. UK universities view students as customers and their parents rightly expect a certain level of service and quality since they are paying for it. However, Mathieson asserted that universities should not pay attention to student experience simply because they are paying customers. Instead, universities should provide educational and life-changing experience to students, according to their fundamental mission.

ON STUDENT EMPOWERMENT

Authentic leaders influence and inspire their followers by revealing their own personal histories and relating their experiences. At the Inauguration Ceremony for New Students on August 27, 2014, Professor Mathieson told students about his own efforts in trying to get into medicine. Mathieson was the first in his family to attend university. Although discouraged by his school career adviser from pursuing a medical career, this made him even more determined to get into medicine. When he applied to University of Bristol's Medical School to do medicine, he was accepted only on the condition that he repeated the Physics A level examination. However, two other London hospitals accepted him into medicine unconditionally. Ironically, he was to become the Dean of the Faculty of Medicine & Dentistry in University of Bristol 20 years later.

Mathieson told this story in order to send the message to students that they should persevere in pursuing their dreams with hard work and determination. They should not allow naysayers to dissuade them from pursuing their life goals but should follow their own inclination and flair to succeed. Universities provide students with the environment and empowerment to make the best of their talents and ambition. He asked students to make the most of their time in HKU. Every day should be an opportunity to learn and living for today and thinking about the future is not mutually exclusive. He wanted students to cherish and seize the opportunity of being accepted into a top university like HKU. They should therefore work hard and benefit from this first-class education to become a responsible citizen.

Mathieson also set a good example of humility and an aptitude for learning in his approach to his job, which is somewhat reminiscent of the Confucius philosophy. In an interview with the Chinese newspaper Ming Pao, he was asked to rate his own performance after two years on the job: he only gave himself a six out of ten, as he had felt that there was room for improvement (Ming Pao June 2016). This kind of down-to-earth approach captures the students' imagination much more than simply preaching to them.

On students' political involvement, Mathieson referred to the comment from a number of commentators that Hong Kong is regarded as the biggest small town in the world: that is, it is a place where politics is influential in everybody's thinking and everything gets politicised. In such a highly-charged environment, students naturally feel the desire to express their political views – in protests, demonstrations, campaigns and civil disobedience. He compared this with the protests against the Vietnam War during his student days. Regarding Occupy Central, Mathieson said that while it was his job to defend the principles of freedom of speech and academic freedom, it was equally important for him to uphold law and order. He cited an incident that occurred in London in 2010 where, after the UK Government introduced university fees, student anti-fees protests turned violent. When the protesters swarmed into the Millbank Tower, the Westminster building that houses the Tory party headquarter, one of the student dropped a fire extinguisher from the roof at the police officers on the ground. The incident could have ended in tragic consequences. Mathieson condemned such violent act as extremely irresponsible and one which deserved punishment.

Mathieson wanted to engage with students and student bodies and be accessible to them. He had developed various channels of communication in order to widen student engagement with himself and his leadership team. He believed that students could come up with good ideas to improve the University. A newsletter –

You Said We Did – first introduced at the University of Bristol, has been used as a platform in HKU to consider students' requests and to communicate whether the University could or could not respond to them and the reasons for those decisions. Mathieson wanted to promote a healthy and vibrant university environment which supports freedom of speech and academic freedom, and a willingness to listen to different viewpoints. He encouraged diversity of opinions. While he supported the students' right to be involved in the Occupy Central movement, he equally supported those students who oppose the movement, believing that both sides have a right to express their viewpoints.

TRANSFORMATIVE EXPERIENTIAL LEARNING

Mathieson was a strong believer in experiential learning through the transformation of the student learning experience. He believed all students should have the chance to participate in experiential and service learning outside HK, in China or other parts of the world. He and his wife had taken part in HKU's Project Mingde to help the poor people in Guangxi, part of rural China. He believed that in helping others, one learns about the world and oneself. He encouraged staff and students to engage more with China, in experiential and service learning, research, teaching and industry engagement. The University should be a bridgehead in engaging with China.

HOLISTIC VIEW OF SUSTAINABILITY

Mathieson reaffirmed the University's commitment to the United Nations' Sustainability Goals. He believed that we should consider ourselves guardians of the planet, taking care to preserve the environment and cultural histories. Likewise, we should all take a long term view of the University, nurture and treasure the University's history and its continuity. We should regard ourselves as transient visitors, and see it as our job to nurture the University for future generations. Mathieson admitted that the University needs to contribute more to society and engage more with industry, as well as translate more of its research into applications and tangible outcomes.

IN DEFENCE OF HKU STUDENTS

On encountering a donor who complained about HKU students being involved with student protests, Mathieson came emphatically to their defence. He said that he had been most impressed by the quality and standards of HKU students through his own teaching experience in HKU. He cited the examples of the recent visits to universities in UK (University of Cambridge, University of Oxford, University College London, Kings College and Imperial College), the HKU students made such a good impression that these top UK universities wanted to develop joint and dual degrees with HKU. Mathieson cautioned against talking down HKU students; instead, we should spread this positive message of our students. In fact, the HKU staff, students and alumni should be lifelong ambassadors of the University. As a footnote, the University had received $1.244 billion from the Hong Kong Jockey Club in 2017, the largest donation in the University's 106 year history.

GENDER EQUITY

Gender equity is a critical issue for universities in the 21st century. Many Western universities fail to fully incorporate women into their most senior structures, and a radical solution is needed. Professor Mathieson is an enthusiastic supporter of gender equity. HKU is a committed member of the UN campaign HeForShe, which promotes awareness and stimulates action to eliminate all forms of discrimination against women. He lent his support to the hands-on workshop Girls4Tech, which works with secondary school girls in computational thinking to help them aspire to and develop a career in the tech sector. Mathieson also said that universities need to do more to promote women in senior leadership positions, given that Hong Kong only has eight per cent of leadership positions in UGC-funded universities being occupied by women. He himself promoted Professor Terry Au to the position of Vice-President and Pro-Vice-Chancellor (Academic Staffing and Resources) in January 2016. Mathieson also wanted to promote women entrepreneurs, and HKU should provide the right environment to harness the energy, creativity and entrepreneurship of women. Furthermore, as part of the gender diversity initiative, HKU has created five annual scholarships to sponsor female students from countries with the weakest economic development based on the United Nations classification, to study at HKU.

Writing in the World Economic Forum Agenda in March 2016, "Women and work: observations on the UK and Hong Kong", Mathieson lamented the under-representation of female leadership in universities. While he conceded that men had been part of the problem, he felt that it is now incumbent on men to be part of the solution. He was very proud to have been asked to become one of the ten university presidents worldwide to be impact champions for UN Women's HeForShe campaign, which encourages men in senior leadership positions to speak out on gender inequity issues and actively do something about it. Matheson has said that "universities should be leaders of society, pinnacles of equity".

ENTREPRENEURSHIP

As worldwide unemployment rises, entrepreneurship education is needed to encourage young people to consider a career as an entrepreneur and to be self-employed. At the Inaugural Forum of HKU's Entrepreneurship Dreamcatchers

Project, Mathieson invited the sixty-seven speakers to share their success and failure stories with the students. He encouraged the students to aspire to be the next Mark Zuckerberg or Pony Ma. The Dreamcatchers Project was created to harness students' energy, intelligence and capacity for hard work in pursuing their dreams. He reassured the students that it is fine to fail and to learn lessons from failures. He observed that Hong Kong needs to do more to promote entrepreneurship, as its innovation system is a little fragmented. With the move of Hong Kong's industries to China, all universities in Hong Kong need to work harder on advancing entrepreneurship, encouraging a willingness to fail and learn from one's mistakes rather than focusing solely on success. Due to the fact that HKU graduates have almost full employability (99.7%) within six months of graduation, it is not conducive for students to take risks. Conversely, it could be argued that since the HKU graduates have almost guaranteed employability, they could afford to take more risks to explore, discover and innovate. Mathieson also reminded students of the immense opportunity that the huge market of China represents.

VISIONARY LEADERSHIP

Visionary leaders have the imagination, foresight and courage to help chart an organization's future. They present a shared vision to bring diverse people together for a shared purpose. They have the forward planning skills to convince their followers that the shared vision is the right direction for the organization. They use positive psychological capital such as hope, optimism, confidence, and resilience to help others to adapt, to motivate them into action.

Under Mathieson's leadership, HKU has renewed its vision for the next decade, 2016-2025. The focus is on the 3+1 **Is** – *Internationalisation, Innovation, Interdisciplinarity and Impact*. These four features translate into promoting global citizenship and being internationally competitive. The University is planning to provide all students with at least one mainland China and one overseas learning experience by 2022. While innovation is on almost every university's agenda, HKU emphasises the concept of *Interdisciplinarity* "by bringing together different and divergent minds to drive and catalyse new ways of thinking, new ideas and concepts and new ways of doing things" (HKU The Next Decade - Our vision for 2016-2025). The idea is that these three combined strategies will result in high-impact solutions to regional and global problems. In this era of the Fourth Industrial Revolution, interdisciplinary and collaboration are essential for innovation (Mezied 2016). HKU's vision is underpinned by three pillars: **Teaching & Learning, Research and Knowledge Exchange**. The strategic framework of **Internationalisation, Innovation, Interdisciplinarity and Impact** is interwoven into these three pillars. This ultimately translates into international curricula, a cosmopolitan campus, and nurturing thinkers and leaders with a global mindset, possessing both diverse knowledge and cultural agility. The Common Core Curriculum includes interdisciplinary and multidisciplinary teaching and learning. Innovation and entrepreneurship are encouraged and nurtured by a number of initiatives including the HKU Dreamcatchers, where students, alumni and friends of the University could meet to explore new ideas and pursue collaborative projects. Research and Knowledge Exchange form the second and third pillars of the strategic framework to promote knowledge creation, translation, realisation and application, and ultimately, high-impact research outcomes.

The overall vision of HKU is to be Asia's Global University, "an English-medium, research-led, comprehensive university providing world-class, campus-based education in a wide range of academic disciplines to outstanding students", with "a "distinct Asian perspective", taking advantage of Hong Kong's special relationship with China. The missions of the University are to create opportunities for its talented students, to advance human knowledge, to serve the needs of Hong Kong, and to make a positive impact on the region and the wider world. Apart from the pursuit of excellence, global outlook, optimism, sustainability and social responsibility are embedded in the curriculum to ensure its graduates serve the society and promote positive social change. The University's vision is built on its illustrious heritage and reaffirms its commitment to the core values of academic freedom and the highest standards of corporate and academic governance. HKU's Vision 2025 is Mathieson's platform to bring polarised groups in the HKU community together, to serve the greater good of the University. He has widely promoted the HKU Vision 2025 in order to mobilize major stakeholders into a shared vision for the University.

In conclusion, Mathieson's leadership was exemplary in that it was underpinned by passion, personal conviction, dedication, humility and empathy. He steadfastly upheld the principles of the academic mission. This kind of leadership is a combination of instinct, experience, beliefs and values (Nelson 2008). The key elements of an authentic leader include understanding one's purpose, practicing solid values, leading with one's heart, establishing connected relationships, and demonstrating self-discipline (George 2003). In the complex case of HKU, there is no guarantee that a leader placed in such a difficult position and under such sensitive circumstances would lead in a well-grounded manner. But Professor Mathieson's astute handling of the student protests and the way he steered the University through turbulent political years in Hong Kong are a lesson for those interested in university presidency. Such authentic leadership is a rarity, but it is exactly the kind of leadership we need for universities to survive in the 21ˢᵗ century.

As a footnote, since the completion of the case study, Professor Mathieson has subsequently taken up the position of Principal and Vice-Chancellor of the University of Edinburgh in February 2018. He will lead one of the oldest and most distinguished universities in the world.

BIBLIOGRAPHY

ACTA (2017) How Much is Too Much? Controlling Administrative Costs through Effective Oversight. A Guide for Higher Education Trustees. *The American Council of Trustees and Alumni, Institute for Effective Governance* July 2017.

Adams, R. and Mason, R. (2017) Tuition fee repayment earnings threshold to rise to £25,000. *The Guardian.* 1 October 2017 https://www.theguardian.com/education/2017/oct/01/tuition-fee-repayment-earnings-threshold-rise-to-25000 [last accessed 2 February 2018].

Aedy, R., Gittens, R., Norton, A., Schleicher, A., and Wolf, A. (2017) Are universities worth it? *Australian Broadcasting Corporation Radio National The Money*, 5 October 2017 http://www.abc.net.au/radionational/programs/themoney/are-universities-worth-it/9018520 [last accessed 16 December 2017].

Aghina, W., De Smet, A., and Weerda, K. (2015) Agility: It rhymes with stability. *McKinsey Quarterly.* December 2015 https://www.mckinsey.com/business-functions/.../our.../agility-it-rhymes-with-stability [last accessed 29 December 2017].

Archibald, R.B. and Feldman, D.H. (2008) Explaining increases in higher education costs. *The Journal of Higher Education*, 79:3, 268-295. [http://dx.doi.org/10.1080/00221546.2008.11772099]

Arnett, A.A. (2017) Republicans overall disenchanted with Higher Ed, *Education Dive*, 11 July 2017.

Arum, R. and Roksa, J. (2011) *Academically Adrift: Limited Learning on College Campuses.* University of Chicago Press, Chicago, USA.

Australian Parliamentary Inquiry into the Higher Education Legislation Amendment Bill (No.3) 2004 - Chapter 3 - University Governance and management issues. http://www.aph.gov.au/Parliamentary_Business/Committees/Senate/Education_Employment_and_Workplace_Relations/Completed_inquiries/2002-04/highed2003/report/c03 [last accessed 23 December 2017].

Australian Government Department of Education (2017) https://www.education.gov.au/ [last accessed 29 November 2017].

Australian Government (2017) Higher Education Reform Package - Student Overview https://www.education.gov.au/higher-education-reform-package-student-overview [last accessed 12 March 2018].

Belardi, B. (2015) *McGraw-Hill Education 2015 Workforce Readiness Survey.* McGraw-Hill https://www.mheducation.com/news-media/press-releases/mcgraw-hill-education-2015-workforcereadiness-survey.htm [last accessed 19 March 2018].

Benderly, B.F. (2018) A trend toward transparency for Ph.D. career outcomes? *Science.* March 7, http://www.sciencemag.org/careers/2018/03/trend-toward-transparency-phd-career-outcomes [last accessed 3 July 2018].

Bently, P.J. (2017) The limits of artificial intelligence. *Financial Times.* 24 May. https://www.ft.com/content/e138a1fd-8f2d-4546-8cec-d5609fea21c1 [last accessed 13 January 2018].

Blank, R., Daniels, R.J., Gilliland, G., Gutmann, A., Hawgood, S., A. Hrabowski, F.A., Pollack, M.E., PriceV., Reif, L.R. and Schlissel, M.S. (2017) A new data effort to inform career choices in biomedicine. *Science.* 358: 6369, pp. 1388-1389.

[http://dx.doi.org/10.1126/science.aar4638] [PMID: 29242335]

Bonde, M.T., Makransky, G., Wandall, J., Larsen, M. V., Morsing, M., Jarmer, H. and Sommer, M.O.A. (2014) Improving biotech education through gamified laboratory simulations. *Nature Biotechnology* 32: 7 pp. 694-497.
[http://dx.doi.org/10.1038/nbt.2955]

Busteed, B. (2015) America's "No Confidence" Vote on College Grads' Work Readiness, *Gallup*, 24 April 2015   http://news.gallup.com/opinion/gallup/182867/america-no-confidence-vote-college-grads-work-readiness.aspx [last accessed 19 March 2018].

Choudaha, R. and van Rest, E. (2018) *Envisioning the Pathways to 2030: Megatrends Shaping the Future of Global Higher Education and International Student Mobility.* https://www.studyportals.com/2018-megatrends-higher-education [last accessed 28 January 2018].

BBC (2017) Is the Knowledge Factory broken? *The Inquiry*, November 2017. http://www.bbc.co.uk/ programmes/w3csvsy8 [last accessed 12 November 2017]

Barnett, R. (2000) *Realising the University in an Age of Supercomplexity*, Society for Research into Higher Education and Open University press, Buckingham, UK.

Barnett, R. (2011). *Being a University*, Abingdon and New York: Routledge.

Belkin, D. (2017) Exclusive Test Data: Many Colleges Fail to Improve Critical-Thinking Skills. *The Wall Street Journal.* 5 June https://www.wsj.com/articles/exclusive-test-data-many-colleges-fail-to- improve-critical-thinking-skills-1496686662 [last accessed 19 February 2018].

Bessen, J. (2014) Employers Aren't Just Whining – the "Skills Gap" Is Real. *Harvard Business Review*, 25 August https://hbr.org/2014/08/employers-arent-just-whining-the-skills-gap-is-real.

Birmingham, S. (2017) Sustainability and excellence in higher education. *Australian Government* https:// ministers.education.gov.au/birmingham/sustainability-and-excellence-higher-education [last accessed 12 March 2018].

Bleiklie, I. and Koga, M. (2007) Organization and Governance of Universities, *Higher Education Policy*, 20, 477-493.
[http://dx.doi.org/10.1057/palgrave.hep.8300167]

Boffey, D. (2013) Language teaching crisis as 40% of university departments face closure, *The Guardian,* 23 August http://www.theguardian.com/education/2013/aug/17/languageteachingcrisisuniversitiesclosure [last accessed 3 October 2015].

Bokor, J. (2012) *University of the Future*, Ernst and Young http://www.ey.com/Publication/vwLUAssets/ University_of_the_future/$FILE/University_of_the_future_2012.pdf [last accessed 3 June 2015].

Bolton, R. (2018) Universities have money to spare: Education Minister Simon Birmingham. *The Australian Financial Review.* 24 January http://www.afr.com/ news/policy/education/unis-have-money-to-spare-says-simon-birmingham-20180123-h0mr7q#ixzz55v5UsIfH [last accessed 2 February 2018].

Botelho, E.L., Rosenkoetter, P. K., Kincaid, S. and Wang, D. (2017) What Sets Successful CEOs Apart, *Harvard Business Review,* May - June, pp. 70-77.

Bowen, H.R. (1981) The Costs of Higher Education: How Much Do Colleges and Universities Spend Per Student and How Much Should They Spend? *The Carnegie Council Series Volume:* 32: 5, pp. 57-58.

Brennan, J. A. and Stern, E. K. (2017) Leading a campus through crisis: The role of college and university presidents. *Journal of Education Advancement and Marketing* 2: 2, pp 120 - 134.

Brickhouse, T. C. and Smith, N. D. (1994). *Plato's Socrates*. Oxford University Press, Oxford, United Kingdom.

British Council (2017) *10 trends Transformative changes in higher education*. British Council. June www.britishcouncil.org/education-intelligence [last accessed 20 February 2017].

Bourner, T., Bowden, R., and Laing, S. (2001). Professional doctorates in England. *Studies in Higher Education*, 26 (1): 65-83.
[http://dx.doi.org/10.1080/03075070124819]

Burnett, K. (2016) Universities are becoming like mechanical nightingales: Sir Keith Burnett reflects on the future of academia and innovation in the UK and China, *Times Higher Education* https://www.timeshighereducation.com/blog/universities-are-becoming-mechanical-nightingales [last accessed 28 February 2018].

Burnett, K. (2018) I see an academic empire rising in China, and the West should take note. *Times Higher Education* https://www.timeshighereducation.com/blog/i-see-academic-empire-rising-china-and-west-should-take-note (Last accessed 2 March 2018].

Calderon, A. (2017) What 15 years of global ranking says about HE trends. *University World News Global Edition*, 1 September, Issue 472.

Cann, O. (2016) Five Million Jobs by 2020: the Real Challenge of the Fourth Industrial Revolution, *World Economic Forum* https://www.weforum.org/press/2016/01/five-million-jobs-by-2020-the-real-chall-enge-of-the-fourth-industrial-revolution/ [last accessed 29 December 2017].

Caplan, B. (2018) *The Case against Education: Why the Education System Is a Waste of Time and Money*. Princeton University Press, New Jersey, USA.
[http://dx.doi.org/10.23943/9781400889327]

Carter, J. (2016) Office Hours: Miami U President Gregory Crawford discusses value of liberal arts education. *Education Dive*, 22 December http://www.educationdive.com/news/office-hours-miami-u-presi-dent-gregory-crawford-discusses-value-of-liberal/432571/ [last accessed 11 March 2018].

C-BERT Cross-Border Education Research Team (2017) C-BERT Branch Campus Listing. (Data originally collected by Kevin Kinser and Jason E. Lane) http://www.globalhighered.org/branchcampuses.php [last accessed 18 November 2017].

Chakhoyan, A. (2017) Is the age of management over? *World Economic Forum*, 7 December https://www.weforum.org/agenda/2017/12/is-management-era-over/ [last accessed 15 December 2017].

Chatlani, S. (2018) Higher Ed critical to Amazon's success - and institutions joining cities to lobby for new $5B HQ, *Education Dive*, 19 January https://www.educationdive.com/news/higher-ed-will-be-critic-l-to-amazons-success-and-institutions-are-joini/510110/ [last accessed 11 February 2018].

Chatlani, S. (2018b) Higher Ed must answer the sticky questions in society. *Education Dive*. 16 March https://www.educationdive.com/news/higher-ed-must-answer-the-sticky.../518955/ [last accessed 2018].

Chen, L. (2014) Beyond The Umbrella Movement: Hong Kong's Struggle with Inequality in 8 Charts, *Forbes Magazine*, 8 October http://w ww.forbes.com/sites/liyanchen/2014/10/08/beyond-the-umbrel-a-revolution-hong-kongs-struggle-with-inequality-in-8-charts/#6aabcf9650b6 [last accessed 30 July 2016].

Chen, Z., Alcorn, B., Christensen, G., Eriksson, N., Koller, D. and Emanuel, E. J. (2015) Who's Benefiting from MOOCs, and Why, *Harvard Business Review*, September https://hbr.org/2015/09/whos-benefitin--from-moocs-and-why [last accessed 3 October 2015].

Chesbrough, H. (2003) *Open Innovation: The New Imperative for Creating and Profiting from Technology.* Cambridge, MA: Harvard Business School Press.

Chesbrough, H. (2006) *Open Business Models.* Cambridge, MA: Harvard Business School Press.

Chesbrough, H. (2012) Open Innovation: Where We've Been and Where We're Going. *Research-Technology Management* July-August Special Issue: Open Innovation Revisited, pp. 20-27.

Chow, C. (2013) *Mission Possible? An analysis of Australian universities' missions.* http://trove.nla.gov.au/work/179700619?q=Mission+Possible%3F+An+analysis+of+Australian+universities%E2%80%99+missions&c=book&versionId=195579722+199139159 [last accessed 31 December 2017].

Christensen, C, M. (1997) *The Innovator's Dilemma: When New Technologies Cause Great Firms to Fail.* Boston, MA: Harvard Business School Press, USA.

Christensen, C.M. and Eyring, H.J. (2011) *The Innovative University: Changing the DNA of Higher Education from the Inside Out.* Jossey-Bass, New York, USA.

Christensen, C.M. (2014) The Innovative Universities at the Colgate University Symposium on Innovation and Disruption in Higher Education.

Christensen, C.M. (2014) 2014 Harvard IT Summit, Morning Plenary https://www.youtube.com/watch?v=oMIcXGRBPRU [last accessed 19 November 2017].

Christensen, C.M. and van Bever, D.C.M. (2014) The Capitalist's Dilemma. *Harvard Business Review,* 92:6, pp. 60-68.

Clark, B.R. (1983) *The Higher Education System: Academic Organisation in Cross-National Perspective.* Berkeley and Los Angeles: University of California Press.

Clark T (2017) Experts on trial, Headspace #12, Prospect's monthly podcast 14 July https://soundcloud.com/prospect-magazine/headspace-12 [last accessed 6 November 2017].

Clifton, J. (2016) Universities: Disruption Is Coming. *Gallup* http://news.gallup.com/opinion/chairman/191633/universities-disruption-coming.aspx [last accessed 3 January 2018].

Coates, H. (2016) *The Market for Learning: Leading Transparent Higher Education.* Springer, Singapore.

Commonwealth of Australia (2017) Productivity Commission, University Education, Shifting the Dial: 5 year Productivity Review, Supporting Paper No. 7. Canberra.

CUHK (2017) Communications and Public Relations Office Statement by Heads of Universities, 15 September http://www.cpr.cuhk.edu.hk/en/press_detail.php?id=2593&t=statement-by-heads-of-universities [last accessed 26 March 2018] .

Coughlan, S. (2017) University of Bath vice-chancellor quits in pay row. BBC News http://www.bbc.com/news/education-42152743 [last accessed 25 February 2018].

Craig, R. (2017) The Top 10 Higher Education Issues We All Agree On, *Forbes Magazine*, 20 January.

Cyranoski, D., Gilbert, N., Ledford, H., Nayar, A., and Yahia, M. (2011). The PhD factory. The world is producing more PhDs than ever before. Is it time to stop? *Nature*, 472, 21 April 2011, pp. 276-279. [PMID: 21512548]

Davies, A., Fidler, D. and Gorbis, M. (2011) *The Future Work Skills 2020 Report*. http://www.iftf.org/uploads/media/SR-1382A_UPRI_future_work_skills_sm.pdf [last accessed 7 June 2015].

Davis, G. (2017) *The Australian Idea of a University*. Melbourne University Press, Australia.

Deboick, S. (2010) Newman suggests a university's 'soul' lies in the mark it leaves on students, *The Guardian*, 20 October. https://www.theguardian.com/commentisfree/2010/oct/20/john%ADhenry%ADnewman%ADidea%ADuniversity%ADsoul1/6 [last accessed 18 May 2017].

Delanty, G. (2001) *Challenging knowledge: the university in the knowledge society*. Open University Press, Buckingham, United Kingdom.

Dobbs, R., Madgavkar, A., Manyika, J., Woetze,l J., Bughin, J., Labaye, E., Huisman, L.and Kashyap, P. (2016) Poorer Than Their Parents? Flat or Falling Incomes in Advanced Economies, July 2016, *McKinsey Global Institute*.

Drucker, P.F. (1993) *Post-Capitalist Society*. New York: Harper Business.

Economist (2010) Doctoral degrees: The disposable academic, Why doing a PhD is often a waste of time, *The Economist*, December 16, 2010.

Economist (2012) The college-cost calamity: Many American universities are in financial trouble, *The Economist*, 4 August http://www.economist.com/node/21559936 [last accessed 3 October 2013].

Economist (2014) The Future of Universities: The Digital Degree, *The Economist,* 28 June http://www.economist.com/news/briefing/21605899-staid-higher-education-business-about-experience-welcome-earthquake-digital [last accessed 4 June 2015].

Economist (2015b) The Future of Work: There is an App for that. *The Economist,* 3 January http://www.economist.com/news/briefing/21637355-freelance-workers-available-moments-notice-will-reshape-nature-companies-and [last accessed 4 June 2015].

Ellis, Y., Daniels, B. and Jauregui, A. (2010) The effect of multitasking on the grade performance of business students. *Research in Higher Education Journal*, 8, pp. 1-10.

Else, H. (2017) British Prime Minister Seeks 'Credible Alternative' to Universities, *Times Higher Education* 27 January https://www.timeshighereducation.com/news/theresa-may-seek-new-credible-alternative-universities [last accessed 28 February, 2018].

European Commission (2006) Delivering on the modernization agenda for universities: education, research and innovation. COM (2006) 208, Brussels.

Fain P (2017) National enrollments decline for sixth straight year, but at slower rate. Inside HigherEd 20 December https://www.insidehighered.com/news/2017/12/20/national-enrollments-decline-sixth-straight-year-slower-rate?utm_source=Inside+Higher+Ed&utm_campaign=e69b9d8a17-DNU20171220&utm_medium=email&utm_term=0_1fcbc04421-e69b9d8a17-97790489&mc_cid=e69b9d8a17&mc_eid=a14cfb4a9c [last accessed 21 December 2017].

Fanelli, D. (2018) Is science really facing a reproducibility crisis? *Proceedings of the National Academy of Sciences*, 115: 11, pp. 2628-2631.

Featherstone T (2016) What students want from universities, *The Sydney Morning Herald*, 18 August 18http://www.smh.com.au/smallbusiness/managing/theventure/whatstudentswantfromuniversities20160817g qudn1.html [last accessed 9 December 2017].

Fei, X., Shobert, B. and Wong, J. (2016) The Rise of Chinese Innovation in the Life Sciences, *NBR Reports*, April http://www.nbr.org/publications/specialreport/pdf/Free/06032016/SR56_ChinaLifeScience_April2016.pdf [last accessed 7 May 2017].

Fischer, K, (2017) International-Student Enrollment Is Slowing — and It Isn't All Donald Trump's Fault. *The Chronicle of Higher Education*; Washington (Nov 13, 2017).

Ferguson, N. (2012) Civil and Uncivil Societies. *The Reith Lectures*. *BBC* http://www.bbc.co.uk/pro grammes/articles/1n02Kr5c1XCGkZbw8wvbv5s/niall-ferguson-civil-and-uncivil-societies [last accessed 22 February 2018].

Foxx, V. and Feulner E. (2018) Taming The Tuition Tiger. *Washington Times*. 22 January https://edwork force.house.gov/news/documentsingle.aspx?DocumentID=402410 [last accessed 2 February 2018].

Funnell, A., Altbach P., Spicer A., Fitzgerald, R., Scott, P. and Reshef, S. (2017) *Australian Broadcasting Corporation Radio National, Future Tense*, 29 October http://www.abc.net.au/radionational/programs/futuretense/education/9076634 [last accessed 16 December 2017].

Gardner, H. (1993). *Frames of mind: The theory of multiple intelligences*. New York, NY: BasicBooks.

George, B. (2003) *Authentic Leadership: Rediscovering the Secrets to Creating Lasting Value*. Jossey-Bass, New Jersey, USA.

Gilligan, A. (2017) Universities take foreign students ahead of British, The Sunday Times, 6 August https://www.thetimes.co.uk/article/universities-take-foreign-students-ahead-of-british-5nppfw5ks   [last accessed 26 March 2018].

Gillings, M. and Williamson, J. (2015) Universities run as businesses can't pursue genuine learning. The Conversation, 19 June https://theconversation.com/universitiesrunasbusinessescantpursuegenuinelearning 43402 [last accessed 2 February 2017].

Giles, S. (2016) The Most Important Leadership Competencies, According to Leaders Around the World. *Harvard Business Review*. Leadership, 15 March https://hbr.org/2016/03/the-most-important-leaders-ip-competencies-according-to-leaders-around-the-world [last accessed 18 March 2018].

Ginsberg, B. (2011) *The Fall of the Faculty: The Rise of the All-Administrative University and Why It Matters*. Oxford University Press, New York, USA.

Gittens, R. (2017) We've turned our unis into aimless, money-grubbing exploiters of students. *The Sydney Morning Herald*. http://www.smh.com.au/business/comment-and-analysis/weve-turned-our-unis-into-aimless-moneygrubbing-exploiters-of-students-20170916-gyiv0e.html [last accessed 16 December 2017].

Godwin, K.A. and Pickus, N. (2017) Liberal Arts and Sciences Innovation in China: Six Recommendations to Shape the Future, *CIHE Perspectives No.8*, Boston College Center for International Higher Education.

Going Global 2012, *The shape of things to come: higher education global trends and emerging opportunities to 2020*. British Council www.britishcouncil.org/higher-education [last accessed 5 April 2015].

Grace, K., Salvatier, J., Dafoe, A., Zhang, B., and Evans, O. (2017) *When Will AI Exceed Human Performance? Evidence from AI Experts*. Cornell University. arXiv:1705.08807 [last accessed 18 March

2018].

Graduate Careers Australia 2015 http://www.graduatecareers.com.au/wp-content/uploads/2015/12/GCA_GradStats_2015_FINAL.pdf [last accessed 18 March 2018].

Gunn A. (2017) TEF: everything you need to know about the new university rankings. The Conversation. 22 June https://theconversation.com/tef-everything-you-need-to-know-about-the-new-university-rankings-79932 [last accessed 15 March 2018].

Gutierrez. R. (2017) *The University For the Future: Evolutions, Revolutions and Transformations*. Lee Hecht Harrison, Sydney, Australia https://www.aheia.edu.au/cms_uploads/docs/lhh-university-for--he-future.pdf [last accessed 6 March 2018].

Hare, J. (2017) Higher degree of pain for students, *The Australian*, 12 April 2017.

Harris A. (2017) Moody's Downgrades Higher Ed's Outlook From 'Stable' to 'Negative', *The Chronicle of Higher Education*, 5 December, https://www.chronicle.com/article/Moody-s-Downgrades-Higher/241983 [last accessed 16 December 2017].

Harris A. (2018) Outlook for Higher Ed in 2018 Is Bleak, Ratings Agency Says, *The Chronicle of Higher Education,* 23 January.

Head, M.L., Holman, L., Lanfear, R., Kahn, A.T. and Jennions, M.D. (2015) The extent and consequences of P-hacking in science. *PLoS Biol* 13:3.

Heifetz, R. A., Linsky, M., and Grashow, A. (2009). *The practice of adaptive leadership: Tools and tactics for changing your organization and the world*. Cambridge, MA: Harvard Business Press.

Herder-Wynne, F., Amato, R., and Uit de Weerd, F. (2017) *Leadership 4.0: A Review of The Thinking. Research Report*. Oxford Leadership. www.oxfordleadership.com/wp.../OL-Leadership-4.0-–-A-review- of-the-thinking.pdf [last accessed 27 December 2017].

Hill, A.V.S. (2016) Vaccines for Ebola: tackling a market failure Oxford London Lecture 2016.

Hong Kong Education Bureau (http://www.edb.gov.hk/en/edu-system/postsecondary/local-higher-edu/institutions/index.html [last accessed 12 January 2018].

HKU (University of Hong Kong) YouTube videos. [last accessed 12 January 2018]
https://www. youtube.com/watch?v=cbwmxmq26Gs High table speech Chi Sun College HKU
https://www.youtube.com/watch?v=nqGEMf0yRhg HKU DREAMCATCHERS
https://www.youtube.com/watch?v=392rHNuQLHQ Nelson Mandela: Long Walk to Freedom by Professor Peter Mathieson
https://www.youtube.com/ watch?v=2eq58dvlTWg High Table Dinner
https://www.youtube.com/watch?v=3_R7mcrnbxo Why is HKU not in the top 20
https://www.youtube.com/watch?v=8pYOHnRdALw Press meeting with Professor Arthur Li, Chair of HKU Council and Professor Mathieson.

https://www.youtube.com/watch?v=MHcH-GIE_kE
https://www.youtube.com/watch?v=8q_DnHT8Vxc
https://www.youtube.com/watch?v=Km8mlSnlOU4
https://www.youtube.com/watch?v=DiFjC-aGg9E
https://www.youtube.com/watch?v=Jogoq408XPs
https://www.youtube.com/watch?v=DqlEQ3xF9MY
https://www.youtube.com/watch?v=2kceeQvMK30
https://www.youtube.com/watch?v=n3hvWOR3xjw

https://www.youtube.com/watch?v=siF1VDip5ck
https://www.youtube.com/watch?v=Wb21YzYPmik
https://www.youtube.com/watch?v=WXp3Sbz0lrg
https://www.youtube.com/watch?v=kS-qCh1eSH8

Horizon Report (2017) A collaboration between The New Media Consortium and the EDUCAUSE Learning Initiative, http://cdn.nmc.org/media/2017-nmc-horizon-report-he-EN.pdf [last accessed 20 March 2018].

Houghton D (2016) Universities cry poor while vice chancellors make a motza, *The Courier-Mail*, 16 April http://www.couriermail.com.au/news/opinion/opinionuniversitiescrypoorwhilevicechancellorsmakeamotza/newsstory/52b8eea62c6a30d9ae [last accessed 25 June 2017].

Huang F (2017) Double World-Class Project has more ambitious aims, *University World News Global Edition Issue* 476 http://www.universityworldnews.com/article.php?story=2017092913334471&query=futao+ [last accessed 18 November 2017].

Isaacson, W. (2012) The Real Leadership Lessons of Steve Jobs. *Harvard Business Review,* 90(4) April, pp. 92-102.

Jaffee, D.(2013). Building General Education With Hong Kong Characteristics. International Education, Vol. 42 Issue (2) http://trace.tennessee.edu/internationaleducation/vol42/iss2/4 [last accessed 10 March 2018].

Jarvis, P. (2001) *Universities and Corporate Universities*. London: Kogan Page.

Jenvey, N. (2017) UK Tumbles, Asia Rises in THE Employability Ranking. *University World News Global Edition,* Issue 483, 17 November 2017.

Jimenez, J. (2016) There's a research revolution going on in China – and one day it could save your life, *World Economic Forum*, 21 July https://www.weforum.org/agenda/2016/07/theres-a-research-revolut-on-going-on-in-china-and-one-day-it-could-save-your-life/ [last accessed 3 March 2018].

Johansen, R. (2012) *Leaders Make the Future: Ten New Leadership Skills for an Uncertain World*. 2nd Edition San Francisco, ca: Berrett- Koehler.

Kail, E. (2010) Leading effectively in a VUCA environment: C is for complexity. *HBR BlogNetwork*. http://blogs.hbr.org/frontline-leadership/2010/12/leading-effectively-in-avuca html [last accessed 3 March 2018].

Kail, E. (2011). Leading effectively in a VUCA environment: A is for ambiguity. *HBR Blog Network*. http://blogs.hbr.org/frontline- leadership/2011/01/leading-effectively-in-avuca-1.html [last accessed 3 March 2018].

Kaufer, D. (2011) *What can Neuroscience Research Teach Us about Teaching?* University of Berkeley http://gsi.berkeley.edu/gsi-guide-contents/learning-theory-research/neuroscience/ [last accessed 3 March 2018].

Kavanaugh, S. and Strecker, G. (2012) Leading learning in VUCA times: How does a volatile uncertain complex ambiguous context impact strategy? http://www.slideshare.net/humancapitalmedia/920-clo-arielgroupfinalslidesv2 [last accessed 3 March 2018].

Kelderman, E. (2018) In New Budget Proposal, California Higher Ed Gets Modest Funding and a Big Online College. *The Chronicle of Higher Education*. 10 January https://www.chronicle.com/article/In-New-Budg-t-Proposal/242204 [last accessed 19 March 2018].

Kelly, U. (2016) *Economic Impact on the UK of EU Research Funding to UK Universities*, http://www.universitiesuk.ac.uk/policy-andanalysis/reports/Documents/2016/economic-impact-of-eu-researc hfunding-in-uk-universities.pdf [last accessed 8 March 2018].

Kenzner, R. and Johnson, S.S. (1997) Seeing things as they really are, (Peter F. Drucker's predictions; includes related articles) (Cover Story) *Forbes*, 10 March, pp. 122-128.

Ker, I. (2008) Newman on Education Cardinal, Newman Society https://cardinalnewmansociety.org/ category/research/ [last accessed 18 May 2017].

Khomami N (2017) University vice-chancellors' average pay now exceeds £275,000: Union calls for scrutiny of 'fat cat' deals as rising tuition fees burden students with debt. *The Guardian,* 23 February https://www.theguardian.com/education/2017/feb/23/universityvicechancellorsaveragepaynowexceeds27500 0 [last accessed 25 June 2017].

Kinsinger, P. and Walch, K. (2012). *Living and leading in a VUCA world.* Thunderbird University.

KNOWLEDGE@WHARTON (2017) Why AI Is the 'New Electricity'. 7 November, knowledge.wharton. upenn.edu/article/ai-new-electricity/ [last accessed 20 March 2018].

Knott M (2017) Budget 2017: Universities to be hit with funding cuts, student fees to rise. *The Sydney Morning Herald* http://www.smh.com.au/business/federalbudget/budget2017universitiestobehitwith fundingcutsstudentfeestorise20170621gvvqqy.html [last accessed 25 June 2017].

Kotter J. (2016) The Power Of The Story: What Happens When Two Old Friends Come Together. *Forbes* 2 July https://www.forbes.com/sites/johnkotter/2016/07/02/the-power-of-the-story-what-happens-when-two-old-friends-come-together/#239810c862f9 [last accessed 18 March 2018].

Lawrence, K. (2013) Developing Leaders in a VUCA Environment, *University of North Carolina Executive Development*www.execdev.unc.edu [last accessed 26 December 2017].

Lederman, D. and Rivard, R. (2014) A More Nuanced Bill Gates, *Inside Higher Education*, 22 July https://www.insidehighered.com/news/2014/07/22/slightly-more-nuanced-bill-gates-offers-vision-higher-education [last accessed 2 April 2017].

Lederman D (2017) Number of colleges and universities drops sharply amid economic turmoil, *Inside Higher Education*, 19 July https://www.insidehighered.com/news/2017/07/19/number-colleges-a-d-universities-dropssharply-amid-economic-turmoil?width=775&height=500&iframe=true [last accessed 9 December 2017].

Lederman, D. and Seltzer, R. (2017) The Rose-Colored Glasses Come Off: A Survey of Business Officers, *Inside Higher Education*, 28 July https://www.insidehighered.com/news/survey/survey-finds-busine-s-officers-increasingly-considering-more-painful-options# [last accessed 9 December 2017].

Lederman D (2017) Is the public really losing faith in higher education? *Inside Higher Education*, 15 December https://www.insidehighered.com/news/2017/12/15/public-really-losing-faith-higher education? utm_source [last accessed 16 December 2017].

Lee, M.H. (2014) Hong Kong higher education in the 21st century, Hong Kong Teachers' Centre Journal, 13, pp. 15-34.

Lee, M.H. (2018) Researching Higher Education in "Asia's Global Education Hub": Major Themes in Singapore. In: Jung J., Horta H., Yonezawa A. (eds) Researching Higher Education in Asia. Higher Education in Asia: Quality, Excellence and Governance. Springer, Singapore. [http://dx.doi.org/10.1007/978-981-10-4989-7_13]

Le Page, M. (2017) First results of CRISPR gene editing of normal embryos released. *New Scientist.* https://www.newscientist.com/article/2123973-first-results-of-crispr-gene-editing-of-norma--embryos-released/ [last accessed 3 March 2018].

Leonard, D. and Swap, W. (2004) Deep Smarts. *Harvard Business Review* September 2004 Issue pp. 88-97.

Lim I.W., and Miller P.W. (2015) *Overeducation and earnings in the Australian graduate labour market: an application of the Vahey model*, Education Economics. 23:1, 63-83.
[http://dx.doi.org/10.1080/09645292.2013.772954]

Liu, L. (2010) *Conversations on Leadership: Wisdom from Global Management Gurus*. Jossey-Bass, New Jersey, USA.

Liu, M. (2016) Shenzhen Daily 'Hospital succeeds when HKU is not needed' http://www.szdaily.com/content/2016-08/08/content_13696994.htm [last accessed 20 March 2018].

Liu, Z., Cai, Y., Wang, Y., Nie, Y., Zhang, C., Xu, Y., Zhang,X., Lu, Y., Zhanyang Wang, Z., Poo, M.and Sun, Q. (2018) Cloning of Macaque Monkeys by Somatic Cell Nuclear Transfer Cell. Volume 172, Issue 4, pp 881-887.e7.

Macintyre, S.F. (2010) Academic Freedom. In: Peterson, P., Baker, E. and McGaw, B, (Eds), *International Encyclopedia of Education (Third Edition),* Elsevier, http://www.sciencedirect.com/science/reference works/9780080448947 [last accessed 18 November 2011].

Madsen, J.B. and Murtin, F. (2017) British economic growth since 1270: the role of education, *J Econ Growth*, 22: 229-272.
[http://dx.doi.org/10.1007/s10887-017-9145-z]

Mance, H. (2016) Britain has had enough of experts, says Gove. Financial Times. 4 June https://www.ft.com/content/3be49734-29cb-11e6-83e4-abc22d5d108c [last accessed 3 December 2017].

Marshall, S. (2018) Are New Zealand universities underperforming? An analysis of international enrolments in Australian and New Zealand universities 48: 1-18.

Martin, S. and Koob S. F.(2017) Third of university students failing to complete course. *The Australian*, 18 January http://www.theaustralian.com.au/national-affairs/education/third-of-university-students-failing-to-complete-course/news-story/0c70435cf769087881… 1/3 [last accessed 7 November 2017].

Mathieson, P. (2016) Asia University Rankings 2016: Don't lose your head – rankings are but one measure of success. *Times Higher Education.* 20 June https://www.timeshighereducation.com/world-universit--rankings/asia-university-rankings-2016-dont-lose-your-head-rankings-are-but-one-measure-of-success [last accessed 30 March 2018].

Maze, R. (2017) Game Changer: Virtual reality program to transform how students learn about the human body. Colorado State University 15 August, 2017. https://source.colostate.edu/game-changer-virtual-reality-program-transform-students-learn-human-body/ [last accessed 20 March 2018].

McCandliss, B. (2015) The Neuroscience of Learning. Thinking Big About Learning Symposium at Stanford University https://www.youtube.com/watch?v=5_6fezBz9IA&t=230s (Last accessed 16 March 2018].

McChrystal S, Collins T, Silverman D, Fussell C (2015) Team of Teams: New Rules of Engagement for a Complex World. Portfolio/Penguin, New York, USA.

McDonald, J. (2017) China announces goal of AI leadership by 2030. APNews. 21 July https://www.

apnews.com/b43da0d919ee46efb0e185668a2be263/China-announces-goal-of-AI-leadership-by-2030 [last accessed 21 March 2018].

McKinsey Global Institute's (MGI) www.mckinsey.com/mgi.

National Science Foundation. Institution Rankings by total R&D Expenditures https://ncsesdata.nsf.gov/profiles/site?method=rankingBySource&ds=herd [last accessed 8 March 2018].

Nature Index (2018) https://www.natureindex.com/country-outputs/generate/All/global/All/weighted_score [last accessed 3 March 2018].

Nelson, C. (2010) *No University is an Island: Saving Academic Freedom*, New York, USA: New York University Press.

Nelson, S. J. (2008). College and University Presidents: Authentic Leadership Principles and the Navigation of Crisis. In *Secondary Education and Professional Programs Faculty Publications.* Paper 8.

Neves, J. and Hillman, N. (2017) 2017 Student Academic Experience Survey, Higher Education Academy (HEA) and the Higher Education Policy Institute (HEPI), United Kingdom.

Newman (circa 1852) Cardinal Newman's *Idea of a University*http://www.newmanreader.org/works/idea/ [last accessed 18 July 2009].

Newby, H. (2015) Governance in UGC-funded Higher Education Institutions in Hong Kong - Report of the University Grants Committee, September 2015. http://www.ugc.edu.hk/eng/ugc/about/publications/report/report30032016.html [last accessed 30 March 2018].

Niland, J. (2009) Five Year Review of Fit For Purpose. University of Hong Kong. May 2009. http://www.gs.hku.hk/5yearReview.pdf [last accessed 30 March 2018].

Noble, J. (2014)Josh Noble in Hong Kong. *Financial Times*. 21 October 2014 http://www.ft.com/cms/s/0/d123d896-5808-11e4-b47d-00144feab7de.html#axzz4FsP3WKCo [last accessed 18 July 2017].

Norton, A., and Cherastidtham, I. (2015). University fees: What students pay in deregulated markets. *Grattan Institute.*http://grattan.edu.au/wp-content/uploads/2015/08/830-University-Fees.pdf [last accessed 7 December 2917].

OECD (2102) Transferable Skills Training For Researchers: Supporting Career Development and Research http://www.oecd.org/science/transferableskills.htm [last accessed 28 February 2018].

OECD (2015), Education at a Glance 2015: OECD Indicators, OECD Publishing, Paris.

OECD (2016). Education at a Glance 2016. OECD indicators. http://www.keepeek.com/Digital-Asset-Management/oecd/education/education-at-a-glance-2016_eag-2016-en#.WIxD81N97IU#page1 [last accessed 9 January 2018].

OECD (2016), OECD Science, Technology and Innovation Outlook 2016, OECD Publishing, Paris.

OECD (2017), Education at a Glance 2017: OECD Indicators, OECD Publishing, Paris.

Olive, V. (2017) *How much is too much? Cross-subsidies from teaching to research in British Universities.* www.hepi.ac.uk/wp-content/.../HEPI-How-much-is-too-much-Report-100-FINAL.pdf [last accessed 7 March 2018].

Orr, G. (2017) What can we expect in China in 2018? *McKinsey & Company.* https://www.mckinsey.

com/global-themes/china/what-can-we-expect-in-china-in-2018 [last accessed 6 January 2018].

Paleit, A. (2014) Interview with Peter Mathieson, University of Hong Kong president. *Financial Times,* 7 October http://www.ft.com/cms/s/2/a215ff06283e11e49ea900144feabdc0.html [last accessed 6 December 2017].

Paul, R. (2015). *Leadership Under Fire, Second Edition: The Challenging Role of the Canadian University President.* McGill-Queen's University Press, Canada.

PayScale, Inc. (2016) Leveling Up: How to Win In the Skills Economy. *PayScale and Future Workplace Report*https://www.payscale.com/about/press-releases/payscale-and-future-workplace-releas--2016-workforce-skills-preparedness-report [last accessed 12 November 2017].

Pells R (2017) Elite UK universities found to be second-rate in new Government rankings. *The Independent.* 23 June http://www.independent.co.uk/news/education/educationnews/topukuniversityrankingsgoldsilver bronzeoxfordcambridgeteftteachingexcellence [last accessed 25 June 2017].

Pew Research Center (2017) Sharp Partisan Divisions in Views of National Institutions: Republicans increasingly say colleges have negative impact on U.S. 10 July 2017.

Popenici, S.A,D. and Kerr, S. (2017) Exploring the impact of artificial intelligence on teaching and learning in higher education Research and Practice in Technology Enhanced Learning 12: 22.

Poutré, A., Rorison, J. and Voight, M. (2017) *Limited Means, Limited Options: College Remains Unaffordable for Many Americans*, A Report by Institute For Higher Education Policy Supported By Lumina Foundation.

Presidential Innovation Papers. *Beyond the Inflection Point: Reimagining Business Models for Higher Education* . Presidential Innovation Laboratory white paper series. http://www.acenet.edu/ news-room/Documents/Beyond-the-Inflection-Point-Reimagining-Business-Models-for-Higher-Education.pdf [last accessed 10 March 2018].

Productivity Commission 2017, Shifting the Dial: 5 Year Productivity Review, Report No. 84, Canberra, Australia.

Quintini, G. (2011), Over-Qualified or Under-Skilled: A Review of Existing Literature, OECD Social, Employment and Migration Working Papers, No. 121, OECD Publishing.

Redden, E. (2017) Surveys document declines in international student yield rates. 7 July, *Inside Higher Education* 7 https://www.insidehighered.com/news/2017/07/07/surveys-document-declines-international-stu dent-yield-rates [last accessed 9 December 2017].

Reuben, J.A. (2015) The Future of Liberal Arts at Harvard University. *The Journal of Wild Culture*, 29 June http://www.wildculture.com/article/future%ADliberal%ADarts%ADharvard%ADuniversity/1522 [last accessed 11 March 2018].

Richardson H (2017) Universities could be accused of 'mis-selling courses' *BBC News education*, 8 December http://www.bbc.com/news/education-42264434 [last accessed 16 December 2017].

Riddell J (2014) There is a crisis in universities: It's in teaching undergrads, *The Globe and Mail*, 19 March https://www.theglobeandmail.com/.../education/...undergraduates...universities/article1 [last accessed 30 March 2018].

Schleicher A (2016) China opens a new university every week. *BBC,* 16 March www.bbc.com/news/ business-35776555 [last accessed 30 March 2018].

Schwab, K. (2016) The Fourth Industrial Revolution: What It Means, How To Respond. *World Economic Forum* http://www.weforum.org/agenda/2016/01/the-fourth-industrial-revolution-what-it-means-and-how-to-respond [last accessed 7 January 2018].

Selingo, J.J., Chheng, S. and Clark, C. (2017) Pathway to the university presidency: The Future of Higher Education Leadership. A report by Deloitte's Center for Higher Education Excellence in conjunction with Georgia Tech's Center for 21st Century Universities. 18 April.

Senge, P.M. (1990) *The Fifth Discipline: The Art & Practice of The Learning Organization*, Random House, London.

Sharma, Y. (2016) New minister to continue world-class research project, *University World News* 7 July Issue No:421 http://www.universityworldnews.com/article.php?story=20160707124926674 [last accessed 30 March 2018].

Shukman, D. (2014) China cloning on an 'industrial scale'. *BBC News*, 14 January http://www.bbc.com/news/science-environment-25576718 [last accessed 4 March 2018].

Simons, M. (2007). The 'Renaissance of the University' in the European knowledge society: An exploration of principled and governmental approaches. *Studies in Philosophy and Education*, 26, pp. 433-447. [http://dx.doi.org/10.1007/s11217-007-9054-2]

Sinar, E., Wellins, R., Paese, M., Smith, A. and Watt, B. (2016) *High-Resolution Leadership* Development Dimensions International, Inc., www.ddiworld.com/hirezleadership [last accessed 7 November 2017].

Spicer A (2017) Universities are broke. So let's cut the pointless admin and get back to teaching, *The Guardian*, 21 August https://www.theguardian.com/commentisfree/2017/aug/21/universities-broke-c-t-pointless-admin-teaching [last accessed 6 November 2017].

Stephan, P. (2013) Too many scientists? *Chemistry World*, 23 January https://www.chemistryworld.com/opinion/toomanyscientists/5820.article [last accessed 4 March 2018].

Stone. G., Zimmer, R.J., Issacs, E.D. and Levi, E.H. (2015) *Report of the Committee on Freedom of Expression* University of Chicago https://freeexpression.uchicago.edu/page/report-committee-freed-m-expression [last accessed 20 March 2018].

The Strait Times (2017), 8 junior colleges among 28 schools to be merged April 21 http://www.straitstimes.com/singapore/education/8-junior-colleges-among-28-schools-to-be-merged [last accessed 9 December 2017].

Sutherland, S.R. (2002) *Higher Education in Hong Kong - Report of the University Grants Committee* (March 2002) commissioned by the Secretary for Education and Manpower http://www.ugc.edu.hk/eng/ugc/about/publications/report/her/her.html [last accessed 30 March 2018].

Swinford S and Turner C (2017) University tuition fees are a 'pointless Ponzi scheme Theresa May's former chief of staff says. *The Telegraph*, 17 August http://www.telegraph.co.uk/ education/2017/08/16/university-tuition-fees-pointless-ponzi-scheme-theresa-mays/ [last accessed 9 December 2017].

Szekely, F. and Dossa, Z. (2017) *The Beyond the Triple Bottom Line Eight Steps toward a Sustainable Business Model*. MIT Press, Massachusetts, USA.

Tang, L., Zeng, Y., Du, H., Gong, M., Peng, J., Zhang, B., Lei, M., Zhao, F., Wang, W., Li, X. and Liu, J. (2017). CRISPR/Cas9-mediated gene editing in human zygotes using Cas9 protein. *Molecular Genetics and Genomics*, 292(3): 525-533.

[http://dx.doi.org/10.1007/s00438-017-1299-z] [PMID: 28251317]

Times Higher Education (2018) World University Ranking https://www.timeshighereducation.com/world-university-rankings/2018/worldranking#!/page/0/length/25/sort_by/rank/sort_order/asc/cols/scores [last accessed 9 January 2018].

Timothy, N. (2017) Higher education has become unsustainable and young people know it. Radical change is the only solution, *The Telegraph*, 17 August http://www.telegraph.co.uk/news/ 2017/08/16/higher-education-has-become-unsustainable-young-people-know/ [last accessed 6 November 2017].

Timmermans, K. (2017) The X Factor Competitive Agility. *Accenture Strategy* https://www.accenture.com/.../Accenture-Transcript-X-Factor-Holtmann.pdf [last accessed 12 March 2018].

Timmermans, K. and Abdalla, R. (2017) ZBx: The Zero-Based Mindset Beyond The ZBB Buzz. *Accenture Strategy* https://www.accenture.com/t20180223T175854Z__w__/be-en/_acnmedia/PDF-71/Accenture-ASZBx-Anthem-POV-final.pdf [last accessed 12 March 2018].

Universities UK (2017) Higher Education in Facts and Figures 2017. www.universitiesuk.ac.uk/ facts-an--figures [last accessed 30 March 2018].

Watanabe, T. (2018) UC President Janet Napolitano considers overhauling her office amid political criticism. *Los Angeles Times*. 29 January http://www.latimes.com/local/ education/higher-ed/la-me-uc-president-office-overhaul-20180129-story.html [last accessed 2 February 2018].

Westervelt, E. (2016) Nobel Laureate Carl Wieman's Education Plea: Revolutionize Teaching. *NPR ED* 14 April https://www.npr.org/sections/ed/2016/04/14/465729968/a-nobel-laureates-education-plea-revolutionize-teaching [last accessed 15 March 2018].

1832. Wicherts, J.M., Veldkamp, C.L.S., Augusteijn, H.E.M., Bakker, M. van Aert, R.C.M. and van Assen, M.A.L.M. (2016) Degrees of freedom in planning, running, analyzing, and reporting psychological studies: A checklist to avoid p-hacking. *Front Psychol.*, 7: 12.
[http://dx.doi.org/10.3389/fpsyg.2016.01832] [PMID: 27933012]

Wieman, C. (2015) Finding New Ways to Learn Science. Thinking Big About Learning Symposium at Stanford University https://www.youtube.com/watch?v=oIpcZbAmDOY (Last accessed 16 March 2018].

Wieman, C. (2017) Nobel Laureate Carl Wieman's Education Plea: Revolutionize Teaching: *NPR Ed* NPR http://www.npr.org/sections/ed/2016/04/14/465729968/a-nobel-laureates-education-plea-revolutionize-teaching [Last accessed 16 March 2018].

Wilkens, R. (2017) The Household, Income and Labour Dynamics in Australia (HILDA) Survey, The 12th Annual Statistical Report of the HILDA Survey www.melbourneinstitute.unimelb.edu.au/__data/ assets/pdf_file/.../HILDA-SR-med-res.pdf [last accessed 6 November 2017]World Economic Forum (2016) The Future of Jobs http://reports.weforum.org/future-of-jobs-2016/skills-stability/ [last accessed 18 March 2018].

Wolf A (2017) Degrees of failure: why it's time to reconsider how we run our universities. Prospect Magazine. August 2017 issue https://www.prospectmagazine.co.uk/magazine/degrees-of-failure-do-universities-actually-do-any-good [last accessed 12 November 2017].

Wolf A, Sellen P and Dominguez-Reig G, (2016), Remaking Tertiary Education: Can we create a system that is fair and fit for purpose, November 2016, *Education Policy Institute*, King's College London.

World Economic Forum (2017) Accelerating Workforce Reskilling for the Fourth Industrial Revolution: An Agenda for Leaders to Shape the Future of Education, Gender and Work. White Paper. *World Economic*

Forum. July https://www.weforum.org/whitepapers/accelerating-workforce-reskilling-for-the-fourth-industrial-revolution [last accessed 29 December 2017].

World Intellectual Property Organisation (2017) http://www.wipo.int/ipstats/en/statistics/country_profile/profile.jsp?code=CN [last accessed 3 March 2018].

Zhang, F. and Zhou, J. (2017) What's next for pharma innovation in China. *McKinsey Global Institute*. September https://www.mckinsey.com/~/media/McKinsey/Industries/Pharmaceuticals%20and%20Medical%20Products/Our%20Insights/Whats%20next%20for%20pharma%20innovation%20in%20China/Whats-next-for-pharma- innovation-in-China.ashx [last accessed 3 March 2018].

Zhao, S. (2014) Occupy Central students and under-fire pollster receive support from HKU's new head - Peter Mathieson, the university's first expatriate chief in a decade, backs peaceful protests, free speech and academic freedom. *South China Morning Post*. 1 April http://www.scmp.com/news/ hong-kong/article/1462367/occupy-central-students-and-under- fire-pollster-receive-support-hkus [last accessed 30 March 2018].

SUBJECT INDEX

Lightning Source UK Ltd.
Milton Keynes UK
UKHW052331150219
337436UK00014B/319/P